ROUTLEDGE LIBRARY EDITIONS:
PSYCHOLOGY OF EDUCATION

Volume 46

SECONDARY SCHOOL SELECTION

SECONDARY SCHOOL SELECTION

A British Psychological Society Inquiry

Edited by
P.E. VERNON

Routledge
Taylor & Francis Group
LONDON AND NEW YORK

First published in 1957 by Methuen & Co. Ltd

This edition first published in 2018
by Routledge
2 Park Square, Milton Park, Abingdon, Oxon OX14 4RN

and by Routledge
711 Third Avenue, New York, NY 10017

Routledge is an imprint of the Taylor & Francis Group, an informa business

British Library Cataloguing in Publication Data
A catalogue record for this book is available from the British Library

ISBN: 978-1-138-24157-2 (Set)
ISBN: 978-1-315-10703-5 (Set) (ebk)
ISBN: 978-1-138-63688-0 (Volume 46) (hbk)
ISBN: 978-1-315-20567-0 (Volume 46) (ebk)

Publisher's Note
The publisher has gone to great lengths to ensure the quality of this reprint but points out that some imperfections in the original copies may be apparent.

Disclaimer
The publisher has made every effort to trace copyright holders and would welcome correspondence from those they have been unable to trace.

SECONDARY SCHOOL SELECTION

A British Psychological Society Inquiry

edited by

P. E. VERNON
M.A., PH.D., D.SC.

METHUEN & CO LTD
36 ESSEX STREET · LONDON WC2

First published 1957

CATALOGUE NO. 5978/U

PRINTED IN GREAT BRITAIN
BY WYMAN AND SONS LTD, FAKENHAM

Contents

Preface

ANY REFORM involves a period of change and adjustment. The Education Act of 1944 envisaged the provision of secondary education for all children. Largely for historical reasons, one type of secondary education, which is normally provided by the grammar school and which gives access to the universities and other avenues of professional training, enjoys much greater prestige than any other. It was inevitable in the absence of provision at this level for every aspirant, and with the strain for the majority of parents in meeting the costs of fee-paying secondary schools, that competition for places should arise and with it the need for some form of selection. In some American and Australian states, where the prestige of the grammar-school type of secondary education is not so entrenched and alternative forms of free, secondary education are well-established and in good repute, the issue for parents is not nearly so acute; but in Britain, with its complex social history, the post-war conditions, and the very natural desire of parents to ensure within their means the best opportunities for their children, have helped to make the process of selection for secondary education a matter of genuine concern and, in many cases, of anxiety.

The problem is not a simple one. With the psychological aspects many features of a sociological, economic and administrative kind are very closely interwoven. If the assumption is made that the methods of assessing success within the grammar school are valid and a good indication of later success, the problem of selection at the age of 11+ is essentially one of predicting such future success and it is possible that previous success, while highly relevant to prognosis, may not be the perfect indication of the child's potentialities. It must be remembered, too, in view of the complexity of the environmental, emotional and intellectual considerations involved and the difficulty of assessing them accurately in all individual cases, that some errors will occur in any system of selection applied to human beings and that, unless there is appreciable administrative elasticity, there will always be unfortunate borderline cases with consequent frustration for the individuals concerned. The best vindication available for any system of selection is that it admits of fewer errors than would occur with other methods. There is always, of course, the separate question of whether or not the philosophy of education and associated administrative organization should be one which calls for selection; but clearly the situation obtaining in post-war Britain has called at the end of the primary stage for some estimate of the child's potentialities. Very naturally many educational authorities have tended to include among the criteria for selection, tests which are designed as far as possible to give an indication of innate ability as distinguished from present scholastic performance which may reflect different degrees of educational opportunity and encouragement.

In view of the natural concern of many parents and the spate of misleading and often emotionally-toned writing on the topic, the British Psychological Society has decided that it would be in the public interest to set down what is known on the various aspects of the problem and to indicate directions in which researches are proceeding. It is hoped that such a statement will result in better informed discussions of the issues in the difficult period usually associated with educational reforms. It should be quite clear that this memorandum is not intended to be a vindication of the *status quo*. The aim is to provide a review of the relevant information, so that interested persons may be able to distinguish actual research findings from statements associated with supposition, prejudice and self-interest, and avoid some of the confusions which arise when questions which are fundamentally economic or administrative are addressed to psychologists. For the problem has many facets and it would seem appropriate in a brief prefatory statement that some of them should be adumbrated.

For many persons of liberal outlook, there is something disturbing in making decisions about the lives of others, and particularly at such an early age as eleven years. Yet at the present time, many parents recognize that something approaching an irrevocable decision affecting the future course of the child's life is involved in directing him to a particular type of secondary school. The procedure appears to allow insufficient scope for self-determination, irregularities of development, and the virtues of persistence and fortitude in the face of set-backs which are much commended in British education. These objections appear to be thrown into sharper relief if it is recalled that, in some areas, an important part of the data for selection is obtained on one or a few school-days when, in view of the suggested variability of some children's performance, a particular child may not do himself full justice. Selection on the basis of school record cards is sometimes used; but the difficulty of equating performances in different schools is admitted and the advantages of comparisons on the basis of standardized tests is lost.

Some observers have maintained that the school year in which the selection is made is often one of strain for all concerned. It appears to be altogether wrong that the education of the young should not be associated with enjoyment. It seems particularly unfair that because of varying provision of grammar-school places in relation to density of population, the ratio of rejection in different areas varies enormously. The practice of grading or 'streaming' children in classes at an early age on the basis of ability has also been criticized. If children are to learn the ways of democracy or the elementary features of an ethic in which everybody counts, there is a defensible case for allowing them to gain experience and insight by working with children of many grades of ability. On the other hand, the advantages of keener competition and more rapid educational progress with selected classes of a higher and more homogeneous level of ability are often advanced.

Progress at school may also be influenced by conditions in the home. There is some evidence to suggest that children from families where there are many forms of favourable stimulation such as interesting toys, books, travel, good conversation, respect for education and encouragement, do record, as a group, a better performance at school than children of approximately the same ability from less favourable homes. It has been suggested too that children from the more favourable homes have a better chance of completing the secondary courses successfully because of the more sustained support and incentives deriving from a home where education and poise are highly valued, and the financial strain of keeping the children at school until very late in their 'teens does not intrude.

As a matter of historical fact, it was in the attempt to penetrate the masking effect of some of these features of educational advantage deriving from social inequality, that the so-called intelligence tests were first devised. In the early years of this century Binet and Simon were concerned to discover to what extent the educational backwardness of groups of Parisian children was due to lack of schooling or to poor innate ability. This followed the pioneering work of Galton in Britain, who was interested in discovering innate abilities of a high order as well as in the problem of assessing cases of subnormality. In the 1920's Godfrey Thomson, working in the county of Northumberland, was able to show that there were appreciable discrepancies between the attainments of children and what might have been expected from their performance in a test situation which sought to exclude attainment and assess innate ability. Since they are designed to minimize the advantages of differential schooling and preparation, so-called intelligence tests of the type applicable to groups have been included in many procedures of selection in the attempt to be as fair as possible to all candidates. Regrettably, there is evidence of practices designed to defeat these attempts at fairness by special coaching, and subsequent pages will summarize research on the extent to which the performance on a group test of intelligence can be influenced by coaching. There are, also, many aspects of the application of intelligence tests upon which some authoritative statement would be opportune at this time, such as the history and description of types commonly used, theories as to the nature of abilities, methods of test construction, and the constancy of the intelligence quotient over a period of years. Clearly too, since assiduity is an important factor in any task, and intelligence tests are sometimes held to favour the quick and 'slick' candidate, who may not be adequate in preparing an argument or in written expression, there must be some review of the evidence on other selective devices, such as attainment in school examinations, the use of teachers' estimates and the essay.

It is not claimed that final answers will emerge on all of these issues; but it is perhaps not generally appreciated that on many of the relevant topics there exists a literature of careful research; and the present document will fulfil a very useful service if it makes these findings more generally known. Clearly too, among a group of scientific persons, issues must arise for debate when the relevant facts are not fully known and are still under investigation. No attempt is made to conceal that, on some points, differences of opinion or emphasis have arisen and are likely to recur. Moreover, the memorandum cannot represent the views of every member of the British Psychological Society; but the Working Party responsible for its preparation does include some of the members who are most experienced in this field. Their doubts are stated frankly, and the result should be a reasonably authoritative statement of the consensus of psychological research and opinion. A general summary of the whole memorandum, together with a list of the main recommendations, is given in the final chapter.

Most of the members of the Working Party listed below have contributed to one or more chapters and, although it may be apparent that some divergences of outlook remain, all the chapters have been discussed at length till fairly general agreement was reached.

Members of the Working Party

Mr H. G. Armstrong, Educational Psychologist, West Riding, Yorks.

Mr G. Bosomworth, Assistant Director of Education, County of Northumberland.

Miss May Davidson, Consultant Clinical Psychologist, Warneford and Park Hospitals, Oxford.

Dr Charlotte M. Fleming, Reader in Education, University of London Institute of Education.

Dr Hilde T. Himmelweit, Reader in Social Psychology, London School of Economics.

Mr D. McMahon, Senior Lecturer in Psychology and Director of the Applied Psychology Unit, University of Edinburgh.

Prof B. S. Morris, Professor of Education, University of Bristol.

Prof E. A. Peel, Professor of Education, University of Birmingham.

Prof F. V. Smith, Professor of Psychology, University of Durham.

Mr W. Vickers, formerly Inspector of Schools, Kent Education Committee.

Dr S. Wiseman, Reader in Education and Director of the School of Education, University of Manchester.

Mr H. J. Wright, Educational Psychologist, Southend-on-Sea; Hon. Sec., British Psychological Society's Committee of Professional Psychologists (Mental Health).

Secretary: Dr Doris M. Lee, Lecturer in Mathematics, University of London Institute of Education.

Chairman: Prof P. E. Vernon, Professor of Educational Psychology, University of London Institute of Education.

I

The Background of Selection

THE PRESENT system of selection for secondary education rests to a considerable extent on the work of psychologists —on the advice they gave to the Hadow and Spens Committees, on the weaknesses they have demonstrated in conventional school examinations and teachers' assessments, and on the alternative attainments and intelligence tests they have devised. But although current controversy and criticism often focus upon their contributions, it is entirely false to regard the problems of selection merely as a matter of psychological techniques. The main difficulties are rather social and political in origin; basically they arise from differences in social attitudes among different sections of the community. The background of selection is extremely complex, and it is much easier for the disgruntled parent or teacher to cast the blame on some scapegoat such as the Education Committee, or the psychologist, or the opposite political party, than it is to understand the issues involved. It is only too tempting also for the popular Press to exploit this confusion and to fan the flames of prejudice.

Our Report is concerned with psychological aspects of selection —with its effects on the healthy mental development of children, and with the techniques that can best be employed given the present set-up. It is not our function to suggest reforms in matters of educational policy. In our educational philosophies and political opinions, we probably differ as much among ourselves, and represent as many shades of opinion, as would any randomly chosen set of British university-educated men and women. And for this very reason we hope that our combined views will avoid any strong conservative, leftish, or other bias. But as students of education and of society, we are not unaware of this wider background; and it will be appropriate to begin with a very brief survey. The survey will be confined almost solely to England and Wales and will not attempt even to cover the somewhat different selection problems that occur in Scotland. Doubtless many of the difficulties with which we shall be concerned—such as the unreliability of examinations and their harmful effects on examinees—can commonly be found in many continental and Commonwealth countries and in the U.S.A. But they tend to take a different form in different educational and social contexts; and 'selection at 11+' is indeed a peculiarly English institution.

The Adaptability of English Education. Among the outstanding motifs running through the history of the English educational system are, first, its adaptability, secondly, its diversity, and, thirdly, its division into several main streams catering for different social classes. The system is never static. Though it often lags far behind the aspirations of progressive public opinion, yet it does change continually with changes in social ideals, and is at the moment in process of doing so, in an attempt to catch up with the changes in the structure of society following the war. The Butler Education Act gave us a blueprint for the future of our schools which won unusually unanimous approbation. But it is far from fully implemented (partly because of the country's post-war economic difficulties), and the final picture may well be very different from that expected in 1944. Indeed the problems of selection to which it gave rise were hardly foreseen, and we can be sure that they too will shift in the course of time. History suggests, again, that the solution of these difficulties—like any other educational change—cannot be brought about by a simple ministerial order or Act of Parliament. Many people might subscribe to the Labour party's desire to abolish selection of 11+, if that were possible. But to assume that it could be done by a stroke of the pen is quite unrealistic. Rather we must think in terms of a programme of gradual change which would be acceptable to the schools, the parents, and the many other interests involved.

The Diversity of English Education. By diversity, we mean that the English seem to prefer numerous individualistic streams or types of schooling to the neat, universally applied, systems more common on the continent. State intervention was indeed violently opposed in the 19th century, until the inability of the churches and voluntary bodies to cope with the education of the masses led to the 1870, and eventually the 1902, Acts. Probably one of the underlying causes of the resentment at present-day selection is that it seems to be applied arbitrarily, from the centre, and to disregard the needs of different schools and different families.

During the 19th century, the ancient public boarding and foundation grammar schools were insufficient to meet the demands for advanced education from the new middle class, and there was a large increase in their numbers, and in the dissenting academies and other private schools. Those that have won the highest prestige are nowadays referred to as Headmasters Conference Schools. They are mostly fed at 14 years (sometimes at 11) by pupils from their own or other private preparatory schools.[1] Many of the other grammar schools, while retaining their independent status, became grant-aided in return for admission of a proportion of non-fee-paying pupils, and submission to inspection. Still other private schools, of varying calibre, have sprung up in recent years to provide for children whose parents dislike the state-maintained or Local Authority schools and cannot afford the public schools, or who fail to gain admission to the more reputable grammar schools. In all something like 10% of those receiving full-time education between 9 and 18 years, are attending Direct Grant or independent schools of one kind or another. They still supply nearly half the university populations of Oxford and Cambridge and, probably, a major proportion of the upper professional and business classes.

After 1902 came the even greater growth of municipal, county, or state-maintained grammar schools, which followed much the same academic curriculum as their prototypes, albeit only a tiny percentage of their pupils reached the universities and the great majority left at 16 to 17 or even earlier. Though these charged fees until the passing of the Butler Act, one quarter of their

[1] In addition, nowadays, a very small number of pupils come from the ordinary grammar schools, under the recommendations of the Fleming report.

places were made free in 1907 for scholarship winners from the elementary schools, and in 1920 40%. In the 1930's, 'free' places became 'special' places, with payment according to means. However, several Local Authorities made all places free, and by 1939 —when some 10% of all 11 to 15 year olds were attending these maintained secondary schools—four-fifths of them paid no fees. Yet another strand in the pattern of post-elementary education was provided by the technical and commercial schools, covering some 3% of children (usually from 13 to 16 or 17) of somewhat lower intellectual ability than those in the grammar schools. Also, before the 1944 Act, there were a few selective central or intermediate schools.

Higher Grade schools began under the School Boards of the 1890's, for supplementing the purely elementary education of the church and state schools. From 1902 onwards these developed as senior or central schools in most of the populous areas, though a considerable proportion of children, especially in rural areas, stayed on in the elementary schools until leaving age at 12, later 14 and now 15 years. With the 1944 Act, elementary schools taking children from 5 to 11 were designated primary (infant or junior) schools, and the old senior or non-selective central, and most of the selective central, schools were rechristened modern schools. At the time of writing, a special effort is being made to supply additional modern schools to cater for the remaining one-eighth of pupils who are still educated from 11 to 15 in the all-age or unreorganized elementary schools.

It was the Hadow, Spens and Norwood reports, not the Butler Act which advocated the introduction of the clean break at 11 years and the reduction of this diversity of post-primary schools to three main types—grammar, technical and modern. The authors of the Act envisaged the development of a number of alternative types of secondary-school organization besides this so-called tripartite scheme, namely bilateral (grammar and technical streams, or technical and modern), multi-lateral (several types of course in the one school), comprehensive (taking the whole range of pupils), and school base (three or more distinct schools on the one campus). With the facilities for further education of non-grammar-school pupils after 15, such as day release schemes and the county colleges, we will not attempt to deal.

Thus when the 1944 Act came into force, there were to be found a large variety of post-primary schools of different aims and standards, and different modes of entry. In addition the availability of the several types of schools varied widely in different areas, and varied between the sexes. By 1954 the proportion of grammar-school places of all types was close to 20% in England and 33% in Wales (this may drop somewhat in the next few years as the post-war bulge reaches the secondary schools, though Local Authorities are endeavouring to keep up with the expansion). But it ranged from just over 9% in Gateshead to nearly 39% in Gloucester, and from some 14% in Nottinghamshire and Northumberland to 42% in Westmorland and 60% in Merioneth. Even within a single borough or county there may be quite considerable differences. According to Clegg (1953), the figures for different parts of the West Riding vary from 15 to 40%; and in any one year there are 1,700 children who pass the lowest borderline for selection, but who fail to get places as they would have done had they lived in other parts of the same county.[1] Technical and commercial school provision, again, varies all the way from 0 to 10% in different areas, and is generally lower for girls. Comprehensive and multi- or bi-lateral schools are very few as yet and, as is well known, the introduction of the former (with the consequent restriction in separate grammar-school provision) rests largely on local political views.

Social Class Differentiation. Though our third theme—the effects of social class differences on English educational history—is probably over-emphasized by some left-wing writers, there can

[1] We must be careful to distinguish variations due to numbers of schools available from variations due to differences in the standards of ability among children living in different parts of a borough or county. For example, we are informed that in Kent the proportions of grammar-school places range from approximately 12% to 33% in different areas, but that these figures closely reflect the proportions in each area with I.Q.s of 115 and over. On the other hand, there is likely to be little difference in overall proportions of able children in Kent and in, say, Cornwall; yet the former county had 18½% and the latter 30% of grammar-school places in 1954.

be no doubt of its fundamental importance in the 19th century, and of its persisting influence even at the present time. Up till 1870, education was the prerogative of the well-to-do and a charity to the poor. A tremendous weight of tradition and prejudice had to be overcome before it was accepted as a social service and as the right of every child; and state-provided education still differs considerably in kind (not necessarily in efficiency) from that which is purchased at private independent schools. The curricula of preparatory and public schools are still largely centred round the classical languages, although the original object—the training of men for the church—no longer carries the same weight, and many alternative courses, e.g. scientific, are now pursued by older pupils. The curriculum of the 19th-century church and voluntary schools was almost wholly confined to the 3 R's together with moral instruction which emphasized the virtues of hard work and of keeping to one's proper station in life. The monitorial system allowed huge classes to be educated at minimum cost and with a minimum of trained staff. Cheapness was also a prime consideration with the School Board and Local Authority elementary and higher-grade schools. Some of the latter developed excellent experimental programmes among their older pupils, and this was encouraged by the Hadow Report in 1926; but the majority merely provided a dull continuation of the elementary curriculum to keep the children busy until they went to work.

In between these two mutually exclusive systems came the Foundation and the new L.E.A. grammar schools. Their curricula were at first as academic as that of the public schools, but —drawing many of their pupils from the elementary schools— they did not usually start foreign languages till 12 years, and most of them soon allowed modern languages to displace the previously dominant classics. Apart from the considerable growth of science courses, and the introduction of easier general courses for the poorer streams, there has been little change in the grammar schools to date, despite the large increase in their less academically minded working-class entries.

One of the aims of the Butler Act was to stimulate a new conception of secondary education for the bulk of the population, untrammelled by the demands of the School Certificate or other examinations designed chiefly for university entrance. But though notable experiments have been made by some of the more enterprising modern schools, many appear merely to have carried on the tradition of the higher-grade and central schools, with the added disadvantage of coping for an extra year with bored and resentful adolescents. Some schools have managed to give their brighter pupils an acceptable objective by copying the grammar schools, and getting them to stay on till 16+ and take several subjects in the General Certificate of Education, with good results. Others have introduced vocationally biased courses, technical, commercial, domestic, agricultural, etc., which do seem to the pupils and their parents to possess a greater degree of reality and usefulness.

More important even than the school subjects studied in the different types of school is the vocational qualifications that they provide. A Headmasters Conference School background is still a strong asset for higher executive posts, including civil service administration and commissions in the regular services (though it may well be that the intellectual and character training received, or the 'snob value' of these schools, have less real influence than the qualities of the boys who go to them). A grammar-school education is almost essential for university entrance and for the professions, for teaching, nursing, and most higher clerical jobs. Although many pupils from the grammar schools no doubt take up manual work of some kind, and although there is a considerable trickle from the modern and unreorganized schools into the 'white-collar' class, yet the correlation between schooling and eventual socio-economic grouping is still high, and is probably believed by most parents to be even higher. In other words the 11+ examination does have a very real effect on a pupil's whole vocational career, and much of the attraction of the grammar school to the parent of an 11 year old lies in the presumed security and prestige of the white-collar job to which it is supposed to lead.

We have commented already on the cheapness with which elementary and higher-grade schools were run. Though there have been tremendous developments since 1902, the cost per pupil of teachers' salaries is still much higher in the grammar than in the modern and unreorganized schools. Following the 1944 Act, the cost of buildings and the size of classes were to be the same for all types of secondary school; but this is an ideal rather than an actuality. True, many modern schools have been provided since the war with buildings and facilities far superior to those of some of the older grammar and public schools; but at least as many are still housed in the worst type of urban school. The school staffs who taught, or are teaching, the 'two nations' differ as widely as the curricula and the equipment. In the public and foundation grammar schools practically all are graduates, and until recently the majority came from Oxford or Cambridge. But because of the gulf between the independent and the state systems of education such teachers are not required to be, or are even actively discouraged from being, trained. In the state grammar schools all the senior posts at least are held by graduates who have had a year's training in a university education department beyond their degree (those not so qualified receiving lower salaries). In the early years of this century almost all elementary and higher-grade school teachers had left school at 16 or 17, and many were untrained, except on the job. However by now all the newly recruited staffs of primary, technical and modern schools have had a 2 or 3 years training-college course since leaving school at 17 to 18, though only a small minority have university degrees. We are not, of course, claiming that a degree necessarily improves teaching skill (except perhaps in advanced grammar-school subjects); but the fact that the schools for most working-class children are generally staffed by less well educated and less well paid teachers, usually themselves drawn from lower socio-economic strata, naturally contributes to their lower prestige.

So far then from there being the desired 'parity of esteem' between different types of secondary school, there is a strongly established hierarchy, corresponding closely to the hierarchy of social classes. Despite the greater social mobility of post-war years, most professional and upper business-class parents (unless of pronounced socialist views) feel that they are losing face if they cannot afford to send their sons to Headmasters Conference Schools. The rest of the upper middle-class families similarly prefer one of the direct-grant or older grammar schools to the state grammar schools. To them and to the lower middle classes the failure of their children to achieve a place in any grammar school tends to be regarded as a social disgrace. Before 1944, failure in 'The Scholarship' was less serious since the children could attend the same grammar schools as fee-payers. Now that this is impossible, the parents tend to patronize the smaller private schools, even at considerable financial sacrifice, in order that their children may mix with others of their own class, and not suffer from the supposed stigma of going to a modern school.

Generalization about working-class opinion is more difficult, since evidence is meagre,[1] having little empirical basis. But it would be roughly true to say that a majority of upper working-class parents likewise refuse to regard any education not given in a grammar school as 'secondary', so that there is strong pressure on their children too to 'pass the 11+'. Their interest in a good education for its own sake and as a means to better socio-economic status has probably increased considerably in the past 15 years. Nevertheless some 50% of the population, presumably mostly lower working class, do not put down grammar school as first choice. Indeed in areas where many 11–14-year children are in unreorganized schools, the modern school may seem to them—by comparison—quite a desirable institution. Technical

[1] In a survey of the—not very typical—Watford area, Martin (cf. Glass, 1954) interviewed over 1,400 parents of an 11+ age-group. The secondary schools of first choice were:

Father's Occupation	*Independent*	*Grammar*	*Technical*	*Modern*	*No Preference*
Professional, Managerial	11	82	4	2	2%
Clerical	3	78	10	5	5
Foremen, Travellers, Small Business	3	61	19	9	8
Skilled Manual	1	48	23	17	11
Semi-skilled, Unskilled	1	43	19	24	12
All parents	2	54	19	16	9%

Similar results have been obtained more recently in another area, and are reported in *Social Class and Educational Opportunity* by J. E. Floud, A. H. Halsey and F. M. Martin (Heinemann, 1957).

schools to some extent cut across this hierarchy, but are mostly esteemed in between the grammar and the modern. It should hardly be necessary to add that the reputation of individual schools within each of these categories varies quite widely depending mainly, perhaps, on tradition and on the qualities of the present head, and increasingly upon the physical amenities of modern school buildings and the equipment they offer. It is somewhat early to venture any statement on comprehensive and bi-lateral or multi-lateral schools. Clearly the institution of comprehensive schools in areas where 'real' grammar schools are also accessible by no means eliminates competitive selection at 11+. Yet there is already some research evidence to indicate that parental approval of such schools is growing.

In conclusion, we can see why the Butler Act's scheme for *allocation* according to aptitude and ability has not been realized, and why instead we get highly competitive *selection* at 11 years. At least half of the child population is competing for grammar schools which will accommodate only one-fifth (more in some areas, but less in others). Moreover the middle classes, who are the most vocal and the most likely to pass on complaints and criticisms to the Press and to M.P.s, are put on the same footing as the working classes, and no longer have the alternative of fee-paying, except at expensive private or public schools. It is largely because class-feeling and political bias are so involved that it is so difficult to view the problems of secondary-school selection impartially, or to devise any acceptable solution. At the same time it reinforces the need for more objective research into the effects of different types of schools on children, and on the attitudes of parents and teachers.

II

History and Survey of Present Procedures

BEFORE 1912 the so-called scholarship examination was conducted in a variety of subjects including English, Arithmetic, History, Geography and—sometimes—General Science. But complaints of its cramping effects on the school curriculum led to the recommendation that testing be limited to English and Arithmetic, the content of which was thought to be more or less common to all schools, as well as essential to more advanced studies. In the years immediately after the first world war, therefore, selection was almost invariably based on 'traditional' examination papers in English and Arithmetic.

The origins of the selection procedure with which we are now familiar lie in the Minutes of the Northumberland Education Committee and Reports of the Bradford Education Committee around this period.[1] In 1919 Bradford used tests which had originally been devised by Cyril Burt in their Junior Scholarship Examination. In Northumberland at that time there happened to be a Professor of Education, Godfrey Thomson, a member of the Education Committee, Andrew Messer, and an H.M.I., C. A. Richardson, all of whom knew something about psychological tests and had a strong desire to 'discover able children in Northumberland schools that rarely if ever entered children for the Junior Scholarship Examination'. Their aim was 'to discount the advantages of a large school with individual attention and special coaching', and to devise a 'selection procedure which gave equal, or almost equal, chances to an unprepared candidate'. They

[1] Some group intelligence tests were used experimentally as part of the 'General Paper' in L.C.C. Annual Scholarship Examinations even before 1920 (Cf. Burt, 1921).

hoped that they would go some way towards achieving their aim by using intelligence tests.[1]

The Northumberland Mental Test, an intelligence test devised by Godfrey Thomson, was added to the grammar-school selection procedure and used, in addition to the traditional examination papers, in awarding a small number of free places in the county's grammar schools from 1921. In 1923, Cyril Burt was asked by the Education Committee to devise standardized attainment tests of English and Arithmetic and these were introduced for the first time in the Northumbrian selection procedure in 1925. The aim of these tests was to provide the Education Committee *and* the teachers with information on the schoolchildren's attainment. (The reception of this type of test by the teachers was curiously different from their attitude to the old Elementary Schools Examination which they had fought against because it was associated with 'payment by results'. It appears from contemporary reports that they appreciated the usefulness of the tests, and valued the comparison between their own local standards of attainment and the impartial objective standards provided by the tests.) It was not however until 1932 that the selection procedure was composed entirely of standardized tests of English, Arithmetic and Intelligence, in place of the traditional type of papers.

Considerable efforts were made throughout these early years to improve the scientific basis of the procedure; for example, age allowances were given in all three papers; care was taken to attempt to standardize the marking of the English and Arithmetic traditional papers; all three sets of marks were brought to the same standard deviation; calculations were made, on the basis of follow-up results, of the best weightings for each of the three papers—although, in actual practice, equal weighting was used. In these first few post-war years, Northumberland had reached a point in the rationalization of its selection procedure which was

[1] Characteristic of Godfrey Thomson, and of all who were urging that the new methods be tried out, is this sentence from a lecture he gave at the time, quoted in the *Newcastle Daily Journal*, 27th November, 1921. 'These psychological tests favour the gifted boy with poor advantages, rather than the rich boy with gifted tutors, and are therefore essentially a democratic method of selection.'

not attained by most Local Authorities until another twenty years had passed.

Meanwhile Godfrey Thomson had moved to Edinburgh University and was invited by other Education Authorities to devise tests for their grammar-school selection. From 1925, then, Moray House Tests of intelligence, of English and Arithmetic, began to appear and were used by an increasing number of counties and towns in Britain. By 1954 three-quarters of the Authorities in the United Kingdom were using Moray House tests in their grammar-school selection procedure. Like the early intelligence tests devised by Thomson, and the 1925 standardized attainment tests of Burt, the administration and marking of Moray House Tests needed nothing beyond the competence of every teacher. Marking was in fact automatic and demanded no judgement on the part of the marker, the answer to each item being either right or wrong and each item carrying one point.

Developments up till 1950. Between the wars there was no such thing as an 'average practice' of Local Education Authorities in selecting children for grammar schools. All the following techniques were in use somewhere, singly or in combination: traditional papers in English and Arithmetic; a 'General Paper' which in some cases was a general knowledge test, in other cases approximating to a home-made intelligence test; internal tests in English and Arithmetic set by the primary school; English, Arithmetic and intelligence tests standardized, either before their use, or on the whole age-group during the selection procedure; English, Arithmetic and Intelligence tests neither standardized nor even tried out beforehand; an English essay marked by single examiners or panels of examiners with or without the aid of standardized guides, and marked by 'general impression' or by analytic methods; oral interviews by panels, by single individuals including heads of grammar schools; primary-school reports; primary-school orders of merit; cumulative school records. The picture is kaleidoscopic, with some Local Authorities moving towards the use of standardized techniques and others apparently moving away from them. Furthermore there was large variation in the weight attached to different parts of the procedure; in some areas a minimum qualifying standard was required in intelligence or attainment, but in others scores in all tests were added together to yield a total mark.

The trends, however, in the 1930's were fairly clear: they were towards adding an intelligence test to the procedure, and dropping the traditional papers in English and Arithmetic (particularly essays and long sums), and to the adoption either of the Moray House standardized tests of English, Arithmetic and Intelligence or similar tests devised and standardized by qualified examiners—usually psychologists. It is not surprising that the trends were in this direction because several Reports of the Board of Education were giving (limited) blessing to these standardized psychological tests, and published work was showing that a properly standardized intelligence test could be the best *single* predictor of grammar-school success. Furthermore, investigations into the essay and the essay type of examination paper were almost unanimous in their findings, namely that the marking of such papers was grossly unreliable. (Equally cold water was being thrown on beliefs in the reliability of interview judgements, but interviewers of borderline candidates between the wars do not appear to have been discouraged from continuing to interview.) It was not until McClelland's investigations were reported in 1942 that the potential value as scientific instruments of traditional English and Arithmetic papers (carefully marked) began to be appreciated. However, the trend towards standardized attainment tests was so strong by this time that few Local Authorities appear to have re-adopted traditional attainment papers. Perhaps it was inevitable that the trend should be towards standardized instruments. Those who used interviews, general records, reports and recommendations, traditional papers and essays were usually people who lacked the scientific attitudes and skills necessary for the validation of their procedures: in fact, their data when recorded at all were usually not susceptible to statistical treatment.

Immediately after the second world war the drive towards conformity (as it could be labelled) received a great impetus from the Education Act of 1944, and from the investigations of Emmett and others which showed that correlations with grammar-school success of around 0·8 could be obtained simply by the use of the Moray House battery of tests. Indeed, one of the leading educational psychologists in the country announced that the answers to all the major technical problems in selecting for grammar schools were now known, and that we had the tools for solving any fresh ones which might arise. The general effect of all this was a fairly widespread feeling of confidence, if not of complacency. In more recent years a number of influences have contributed to a more questioning attitude, greater nonconformity and more experimentation. But before taking this up we will try to outline current procedures. Our survey is intentionally brief, since a full account is likely to be published shortly by the National Foundation for Educational Research in England and Wales[1] (Pidgeon and Yates, 1957).

Present Procedures. At the time of writing there is no 'standard practice' which can be taken as typical for the whole country; nor is this surprising when we remember that the Ministry of Education in no way dictates the selection procedure to be adopted. The 1944 Education Act merely enjoins Local Authorities to provide schools 'sufficient in number, character and equipment to afford for all pupils opportunities for education offering such variety of instruction and training as may be desirable in view of their different ages, abilities and aptitudes, and of the different periods for which they may be expected to remain at school'. Thus the techniques employed in diagnosing 'abilities and aptitudes' are left to each Local Authority. Perhaps, however, the following account of the most frequently recurring techniques is not too wide of the mark.

All children who will have reached the age of 11 but not 12 on the 1st September following, take standardized objective tests of Intelligence, English and Arithmetic in their own schools on a fixed day—usually in February. Note therefore that the actual age range on this date is normally 10: 6–11: 5; hence the conventional term 'the 11 plus' is somewhat of a misnomer. Children who are absent on this day are given parallel tests on another day.

[1] Cf. also the valuable unpublished 1951 survey by Dr J. J. B. Dempster: *Selection for Secondary Education.*

Most Authorities also allow pupils from independent schools in the area to take the same tests. The children's own teachers administer the tests, mark them and convert the raw scores into standard scores or quotients. The tests are then sent to the Education Office of the Local Authority, where some checking of the marking is done, and order-of-merit lists are prepared. The order-of-merit is in terms of the total of the three quotients (standard scores).

The Examinations Board (a Sub-Committee of the Secondary Education Committee with representative teachers on it) meets and decides where to draw the line on the order-of-merit list above which all children will go to grammar school without any further consideration. This line will be drawn some way above the point corresponding to the number of grammar-school places available. Another line will be drawn at a point correspondingly below this theoretically exact point. The children whose names appear between these two lines are then called border-zone children, half of whom will eventually be offered grammar-school places.

The Examinations Board (or its subsidiary panels) then examine additional evidence which can throw light on the relative suitability of these border-zone children. Reports previously submitted by heads of primary schools on all the children are scrutinized; special reports may be called for, and particular attention is paid to evidence which enables a comparison to be made between children in the same primary school. As a result of this the Examinations Board will feel reasonably confident that they can now fill the majority of the remaining grammar-school places; they may also feel confident enough to decide against some of the border-zone children.

The last of the places are filled when the Examinations Board have collected additional information on the children who still have a question-mark beside their names; for example, their school exercise books may be looked at, and the heads and class teachers visited at the school; the children may be called to a centre and given additional tests, including essays.

Some Authorities allow over-age children in the primary school a second chance, and some admit under-age children to examination on special recommendation from their head teacher. Children not allocated to grammar school can be reconsidered the following year, with tests appropriate to their age, if the head of the secondary modern school recommends them. Others may be transferred after 2, 3 or 4 years in the modern school.

This can be taken as the general theme, but there are many variations. In some areas there will be not one but two fixed days for testing, the first preceding the second by as much as three months and used to screen off all those—anything up to half the age-group—who are unlikely to be serious candidates for grammar schools. In such cases the Intelligence test may be used as a screen, the attainments tests being given on the later date. Some Examinations Boards set up interviewing panels: sometimes all border-zone children are interviewed, but it is the more usual practice to interview only those still remaining as doubtful cases after all other border-zone procedures have been completed. Another variation—although this is a rare one—is to ignore the three main test results when considering border-zone children and to make the decisions on the basis of the additional evidence only. Some Local Authorities with widely scattered grammar schools have a single county-wide standard of selection by which they judge the suitability of all children for grammar school; other Authorities with the same problem fill up the vacant places in the separate grammar schools with the most suitable children in each separate catchment area, and ignore the ideal of a county-wide standard of suitability.

Variations in selection procedures (as distinct from variations in the proportions of available places) do indeed mean that some children who pass in one area might fail in another. But it would only be asking for further trouble to disregard local needs, and to try to impose some uniform procedure in all areas. Another variation is in the use of specialists to help with the problem. The majority of Local Authorities simply buy standardized tests (Moray House or National Foundation) and depend on their own resources, administrative and teaching, for such technical assistance as they feel to be needed. Others, to a greater or lesser extent, employ psychologists to advise on the procedure, prepare tests, calculate age allowances and advise on border-zone techniques. A few have full-time Selection Officers who, in addition to all this, keep a follow-up going and maintain constant contact with the primary and secondary schools.

All Local Authorities—the bold and the timid, the experimental and the stick-in-the-mud—are trying to perform the task laid on them by the Education Act in a way which is (to borrow a phrase of Alec Rodger's) 'technically sound, administratively convenient and politically defensible'. This is not an easy task. It is quite understandable that many an Education Officer advises his Local Authority to stick to a selection procedure comprising only three Moray House tests. He knows that their technical soundness has been shown by several follow-up studies, and that correlations with grammar-school success higher than 0.85 are almost too much to hope for. He knows that nothing can be more administratively convenient than one or two official testing dates and that the marking of the tests, the conversion to quotients and the preparation of order-of-merit lists present little or no difficulty. He is also aware that it is politically defensible to draw across an order-of-merit list a line which says 'These are in and those are out'. He knows only too well that British citizens have a strong tendency to accept as fair and democratic competitive mark lists even when the same citizens realize that there is no real difference in calibre between someone with 351 and someone else with 352. Small wonder then that many Local Authorities, particularly those with age-groups of ten to twenty thousand or more to cope with, keep their border-zones very narrow, and employ the simplest possible border-zone techniques. Nevertheless—in view of accusations of the completely arbitrary or chancy nature of selection—we would stress the point that every Local Authority does regard it as a serious responsibility, and gives much thought to the most efficient procedure which is appropriate to local conditions and traditions.

Common Defects. At the same time, some of the commonly adopted methods are technically inferior to others, and it would be well to draw attention to them here, while leaving detailed discussion to later chapters.

1. The abolition of standardized tests, particularly of intelligence tests, and reliance on older and more conventional types of examination (e.g. essays), on school reports and interviews, tend

to increase the advantages of the middle-class over the working-class child (cf. Chapters III and VI).

2. These unstandardized methods often ignore age allowances, or make only a guessed allowance without checking whether it over- or under-compensates for age differences. This is serious, since several researches have demonstrated that, when allowances are neglected, the oldest children in an age-group (say the 11:5's) are at least twice as likely to be considered suitable for grammar school by their teachers as the youngest (the 10:6's) (cf. Morley, 1950; Clark, 1956). It is true that the age allowances included in standardized tests often lead the teachers to accuse the tests of penalizing the older child; moreover these older children in fact tend to turn out better in the grammar school. In the first few secondary years, a majority of the C-stream are apt to be the June–September born who have had only 6 years of primary schooling, rather than the September–December born who have had 6½ to 7 years. But despite this advantage, it is manifestly unfair to recommend or admit 26% of the older and 13% of the younger to grammar school, instead of a uniform 20%.

3. Gradings, school marks, or record-card evidence, are often employed without any attempt to adjust the widely varying standards of different junior-school teachers, other than through the general impression of the panels (or of grammar-school heads) that certain schools are habitually too generous, others too modest, in their recommendations (cf. Chapter VIII).

4. In a large Authority, several panels may be needed to cope with the work, and their standards and criteria of judgement are likewise apt to vary widely.

5. The English and Arithmetic papers (and the 'General Knowledge' which is sometimes substituted for an intelligence test) are not adequately tried out beforehand. Often they are too difficult, being suited to the ideal rather than the actual child. Thus their mark distributions are apt to be very irregular; for example they may provide good discrimination of the top 5% of pupils, but be very inefficient in differentiating the top 20% from the rest. No proper weighting scheme is introduced: if each paper is marked out of 100, the chances are that Arithmetic has far more weight in the final total than English.

6. Again, owing to this lack of previous trials, insufficient or unclear instructions are given, and the various supervisors in different primary schools add varying amounts of oral explanation.

7. Though a detailed marking scheme may be issued to the various examiners or panels, it fails to foresee all the possible varieties of answers, and so leaves scope for considerable variations of marking between examiners. The subjectivity of marking of English essays in particular is brought out in Chapter VII, but this applies too to comprehension and other questions in English, and to the assessment of answers to long Arithmetic problems.

8. In an effort to discourage schools from cramming, some examiners set unusual, ingenious and tricky questions. Children's performance at such questions is much more chancy and statistically unreliable than at more standard material with which they are familiar beforehand. Incidentally the content of such questions often tends to favour the urban and middle-class child more than does the content of standard tests.

9. An interview, at least of border-zone pupils, is often included. As shown in Chapter IX, great variations are apt to occur between different interviewing panels, and judgements based on personal appearance and manner, questioning and conversation, might well be reversed by a second panel. Higher social class and age are again likely to be favoured.

Changes and Developments. We should freely admit that by no means all the critics of current objective procedures are obscurantist, or lacking in scientific attitude and skill. In recent years many psychologists have found themselves agreeing with teachers and others who objected both to the influence that the standardized examination was appearing to have on the primary school, and to the possible inaccuracy of relying on the results of a single testing session. They have welcomed experiments with procedures which used cumulative record cards, essays and interviews, and teachers' estimates. The National Foundation for Educational Research, established soon after the war, gave a considerable impetus to this movement by initiating a series of investigations into the prognostic value of different techniques of selection (Pidgeon and Yates, 1957). So far, little validation of these less objective, unstandardized procedures has been reported, with the possible exception of the essay, but this has not prevented the movement towards the holistic approach spreading so that more Local Authorities are using records,[1] giving intelligence and other tests on two or three occasions, reintroducing the essay and the interview.

Those with no love for and no understanding of objective testing procedures were greatly encouraged by the publicizing in 1952 of the influence of coaching and practice on performance in intelligence tests. The long-term effect of this controversy cannot yet be assessed but over a short period it appears to have increased distrust of objective tests. A few Local Authorities have emptied out the baby with the bath water and retreated to a pre-1921 position. Others have ensured that the selection procedure includes more than one intelligence test; sometimes these are given several months, sometimes only days apart. Many Local Authorities are giving increasing weight to non-quantified data, particularly for children in the border-zone, thus implying that, while objective tests are of great usefulness in making decisions on the 'clear-accepts' and the 'clear-rejects', they are less useful in differentiating those in between. In the main it seems true to say that the publicity given to the influence of coaching and practice on performance in intelligence tests has been to stimulate the general trend towards trying to assess the whole child as a person and, especially at the border-zone, to take account of individual quirks and circumstances. Some of these changes may well lead to a lowering of the predictive value of the selection procedures hitherto in use. However, with the psychologists themselves now widening their scope and getting to work on checking the value of these less objective methods, there is hope that their real worth will before long be established.

This Report makes no pretence at setting out an ideal technique of selection. We shall see that every instrument has its merits and its defects, and indeed that there is not a great deal to choose in predictive validity between different instruments, when they

[1] Board of Education (later Ministry of Education) Reports have consistently through the last thirty years urged the use of teachers' reports and cumulative school records.

are applied in a technically sound manner (except for the definite inferiority of the interview). Thus many different combinations of tests, examinations and other methods, are capable of giving highly valid results; while at the same time no combination can ever give anything like perfect prediction.

A Note on Selection for Technical and Commercial Schools. This topic must not be omitted altogether, though we shall not attempt to deal with it in detail, since numbers and types of schools, ages of entry, etc., vary so widely from one area to another, and in many L.E.A.s it is non-existent. Between the wars, technical education for the schoolchild was limited to the junior technical school admitting pupils at 13+. This meant, in practice, selection from those left after the grammar schools had taken the cream at 11+, though in fact quite a proportion of able children, whose parents had refused grammar-school places for financial reasons, did find their way there. Under the 1944 Act technical high schools having equal prestige with the grammar schools were envisaged; but progress in their establishment has been lamentably slow, considering the national need for technicians and technologists. Some Authorities still transfer, after further examination, from modern schools at 13, while some split off technical streams from the grammar entries at this age. Probably a majority now accept at 11+ on the basis of the ordinary selection examination and parents' choice, sometimes supplemented by tests of spatial judgement, mechanical aptitude and interests. These specialized instruments are discussed in Chapter IX. One quite common practice is to draw up a single order-of-merit, and to send the top slice to the grammar schools, and the next slice to technical and/or commercial schools. This naturally means that the latter get only the less able pupils. However there is an increasing tendency to put them on an equal footing, and to apply the same selection standards to both types of school.

III

General Considerations

WE HAVE seen that the underlying causes of the present controversies over selection are primarily historical, administrative and social. Nevertheless there are many aspects of the system which require careful consideration from the psychological standpoint. It may well be that much of the public disquiet is whipped up by politicians and the Press; for the volume of genuine complaints or appeals from parents and teachers to their Local Authorities, or to M.P.s, is nothing like as large as is sometimes supposed. All the same, it would be foolish to deny that widespread criticism from thoughtful people does exist. Indeed psychologists themselves are far from complacent about the situation. The majority of them would probably gladly abolish the selection system if there were a practicable and just alternative. And many have gone so far as to advocate that their profession should 'contract out', and refuse to have anything more to do with procedures that have such harmful effects on children's educational and emotional development (cf. Chapter IV). We believe that this attitude is mistaken—that psychologists have done much to bring about improvements, and can do more. Others have published serious criticisms which deserve a serious answer. Simon (1953), for example, while chiefly expressing the left-wing egalitarian point of view, does make a strong case against many of the assumptions underlying the use of intelligence tests, and the segregation of different streams of pupils in different secondary schools. And Heim (1954), from the more scientific standpoint of the experimental psychologist, points out numerous weaknesses in current testing. We shall show later in this chapter, and in Chapter VI, that we accept some of their arguments, and will attempt to supply reasoned answers to others.

Selection and Social Class. Some of the most widespread criticisms of current selection are that it favours middle as against working-class children, and thus increases class-segregation. Now it is not the business of psychologists to pass judgement on this, or other, policies, except in so far as they are clearly conducive to psychologically desirable or harmful consequences. Psychologists are *not* concerned to advocate either social conservatism or social change. At the same time, together with their colleagues the sociologists, they *are* qualified to investigate the actual effects of various policies. They should, for example, inquire into the extent to which such selection procedures as the intelligence test, or the interview, tend to increase or decrease the mobility of social classes, and to accelerate or frustrate other social changes. Again they are extremely interested in the question of how far comprehensive schooling is effective in breaking down class barriers, though they have not yet had the opportunity of studying this, or related issues, scientifically.

Now in fact the 1944 Act has greatly increased the proportion of working-class children in grammar schools. According to surveys by the London School of Economics,[1] the percentage of children of manual workers rose from 15% to 43% in South-West Hertfordshire between the 1930's and 1951. If selection was based solely on intelligence tests, the over-all proportion would actually reach nearly 60%, as indicated in Chapter VI. And a more recent survey by Floud (1957) shows that, with the abolition of the intelligence test in this area, there has been a small but persistent 'diminution of opportunity for working-class boys and corresponding increase in opportunity for those at the higher social levels'.[2] At the same time it is perfectly true that lower-working class children are still much under-represented. In Halsey and Gardner's study (1953) of four grammar and four modern schools in the London area, between 7 and 20% of the entries to grammar schools, as contrasted with between 30 and 60% of the entries to modern schools, belonged to this class. It

[1] Cf. Footnote, p. 21.

[2] An alternative way of stating the same point is that, even when intelligence test differences between classes are held constant, middle-class children still have a considerable advantage.

is interesting to note that eldest children in working-class families, also those from smaller families, get somewhat more grammar-school places; whereas in middle-class families success in gaining entry is not related to ordinal position or family size, suggesting that the pressure extends to all their children.

Others would argue that such class bias as exists is more than justified by the better achievement of middle-class children in the grammar schools and their—in many ways—better adjustment. There is ample evidence of this from such researches as Campbell's (1952) and Fraser's (1955). Indeed it has been shown that, among children at the selection borderline according to standard Moray House tests, an index of social class provides the best single predictor of future success. Middle-class children are more likely to complete the grammar-school course (cf. Ministry of Education's Report on Early Leaving, 1954). In one survey, for example, children of the professional and managerial class, who constituted some 15% of the child population, filled 25% of grammar-school places and 44% of grammar-school sixth forms. Himmelweit's inquiries (Glass, 1954) show greater acceptance of grammar-school aims among middle-class children, more concern over marks, and more membership of school clubs. They are regarded by their teachers and peers as better mannered and more popular. Middle-class parents pay more visits to the school and give more help with homework.

It would seem to be a fair deduction that most of the factors relevant to secondary-school success are more favourable in middle-class families, including such material conditions as financial support and a private room for homework, etc., also the intellectual standards which help to foster academic abilities, and the emotional climate which emphasizes the value of good education and hard work. Yet at the same time it should be remembered that all these class differences are small, and that there is much overlapping. For example, in response to the question: 'How important do you think good marks at school are for getting on in the world later on?' 76% of middle-class boys answered 'Very important', and the figure of 63% for working-class boys is not much lower. Further, there is already some evidence that, in schools where there is an active policy of continuous friendly contact between teachers and parents throughout the child's grammar-school life, differences in school performance and age of leaving between pupils of similar ability, coming from different socio-economic backgrounds, largely disappear.

Such findings as these tend, of course, to reinforce the socialist critic's views that the selection system and the grammar schools are strongholds of class differentiation, which can be overcome only through the general adoption of comprehensive schools. At the same time they suggest that very many working-class parents accept middle-class values and look on the grammar schools as a means whereby their children can rise in the social scale. Clearly it is not our function to attempt to resolve such issues.

Intellectualistic Bias in Selection. A rather different type of criticism of the selection system is that it puts a premium on an academic type of ability, and fails to provide as good an education for those with other types of ability (particularly of the technical kind), and with the character qualities that make for leadership in our society. The psychologist's tests, it is said, are picking out a 'Moray House élite' of pupils who are best fitted to become clerks, civil servants, teachers and other professionals, and may be keeping down many who would make the best engineers, Army officers, business men and politicians. It is even suggested, with some justification, that selection may have become too efficient in denuding the modern and technical schools of children with high intellectual qualities (thus contributing incidentally to their poor prestige); and that the well-intentioned meddling of the past few decades with the traditional mechanisms by which ability and character came to the top may be conducive to greater social conflict between the intellectual or the bureaucrat on the one hand, and the helot on the other hand. For example, it is removing from the working classes the best intellects who used to become foremen and Trades Union Leaders.

These arguments are, however, highly speculative, and in many respects psychologically debatable. Yet an interesting confirmatory sidelight has been provided by recent researches at Oxford into bodily physique and selection (Davidson *et al.*, 1957). By applying Sheldon's system of somatotyping, adults or children can be classified according to their relative muscular, visceral or cerebral development, and these physical characteristics are believed to be associated with certain temperamental tendencies. The mesomorph or muscular type, for example, tend to be more active, dynamic and practical than do other types. The Oxford workers found that mesomorphic children are sometimes less intellectually developed at 11 years, and therefore do not get a full share of grammar-school places. Yet at the same time mesomorphic adults who do reach the university show excellent intellectual, as well as athletic and other, qualities. Obviously it is difficult to imagine Education Authorities agreeing to consider somatotypes in 11+ selection, and indeed research so far would not justify such a step. But the finding does suggest that more flexible techniques of selection, making greater allowances for temperamental qualities, are needed.

The main weakness in the criticisms we have outlined is that they imply a fallacious picture of mental organization. They assume that intellectual and character qualities are in some sense opposed to one another, or alternatively that academic and technical or practical abilities are antithetical. Such views were implicit in the Norwood Committee's recommendations for three types of secondary school to serve three quite hypothetical types of child; and these have been thoroughly exposed by Burt (1943 *c.*). The fundamental fact is that abilities, together with desirable interests and character traits, tend more often than not to go together. Thus, to a large extent, the children who do best in an academic grammar school are the same as those who would do best in a technical or a modern school. Hence the main basis of any segregation or selection must be general, all-round intellectual ability; and this is what we are, in fact, able to measure fairly effectively at 11 years. Nevertheless, over and above this general ability, there are some children who are more strongly developed on the academic-verbal and others on the technical-practical, side, also some who are relatively more interested in intellectual matters, while others show stronger social and leadership qualities. These are not distinct types, any more than tall and short pupils are separate types; rather they represent opposite ends of a continuous distribution. And it is very difficult to assess such differences accurately, especially at 11 years, although—as shown in Chapter IX—there are some promising psychological techniques for picking out those who have stronger technical than academic interests, or the converse, and even for diagnosing character qualities relevant to school adjustment.

Now although the main basis of selection must be uni- rather than multi-dimensional (i.e. in terms of the level of schooling for which the child is fitted rather than for type of schooling), it would still be entirely feasible to bias our selection in one direction or another. For example, if non-verbal and mechanical tests were substituted for the present mainly linguistic type, we would still pick very largely the same boys as before, but we would get rather more who were suited to a technical or scientific education, and fewer who were best suited to academic schooling. The particular tests or examinations used for selection at the present time are chosen mainly because they give the best predictions of later success in the grammar school or GCE results—as shown in Chapter V. If, however, we decided to adopt a less intellectualistic criterion of 'profiting from secondary education', based for example on assessments of the pupils' social and character traits at 16 years, we would doubtless find changes in the predictive value of our instruments. Thus intelligence tests might turn out to be less useful than ratings provided by the junior schools. In this kind of way, therefore, selection procedure could well be modified in certain directions, though probably at the cost of some loss in accuracy. But it is for society and its educational leaders, not for psychologists, to say whether modifications are desirable, and if so in what direction.

Grouping and Streaming. The above discussion raises the still more fundamental issue of whether any grouping, segregation or selection of pupils is educationally desirable. In so far as each pupil is an unique individual, his education would, presumably, be most effective if it could be planned to suit his particular combination of abilities and qualities. Obviously this is impracticable. Moreover education implies not only the fullest development of each individual, but also the training of different individuals to conform to society's pattern of intellectual and social norms. Hence there is a positive advantage in educating very diverse individuals in groups. Inevitably, then, the individuals within a group such as a school class will be extremely heterogeneous. Now the common experience of teachers is that groups become more manageable and easier to teach if they do not differ too widely in respect of their intellectual and emotional characteristics. Without some systematic grouping, the educational process becomes inefficient from the standpoint of the pupils' progress, and frustrating to all concerned. It would be absurd, for example, to try to train imbecile children and University students of atomic physics in the same group. But how far should the attempt to reduce heterogeneity go, and in what directions should it be sought?

There is general agreement that age, which so largely determines intellectual and emotional maturity, should be reasonably uniform; also physical status—the deaf, the partially sighted, and certain other handicapped groups being segregated. But almost any other type of homogeneity, or criterion of classification, seems to raise difficulties. For example, sex differentiation is highly controversial. A common linguistic background might seem desirable, though it is not always obtained, e.g. in parts of Wales and Scotland. But there would be an outcry if middle-class parents stated openly (what many of them feel) that they do not want their children to attend modern or comprehensive schools partly because the language of the majority of pupils is different from their own. Social class grouping does to a considerable extent serve to differentiate the fee-paying independent schools from the rest, but is debarred as a criterion within the state system. Grouping by attainments and intelligence has been legalized in the 1944 Act's phrase 'ability and aptitude'. Yet it is far from universally accepted, partly because differences in ability to some extent go with differences in social class, and partly because of its implications for family prestige.

Psychologists would argue that if any long-term segregation is to be carried out, it must be based on some stable and enduring characteristic, which can be accurately assessed, and which has a major influence on educational progress. Thus schools for 11–12-year-olds cannot readily be differentiated to cater for different interests or 'types' of mentality, as we have already seen in criticizing the Norwood Report. Whereas by 18–20 years the inclinations and abilities of students for engineering, medical, linguistic and other types of course have been relatively firmly established. Short-term segregation, such as splitting up a class into different groups for number-work, reading, football, etc., or, at a higher level, cross-classification or 'setting' within a secondary school is also entirely reasonable, and conducive to educational efficiency.

Stereotyping Effects of Streaming by Ability. Grouping or streaming by ability constitutes a particularly difficult psychological problem, quite apart from its social implications. Psychologists have often argued in its favour in the past, but their views have modified since research has shown that both the degree of stability of general ability, and the extent to which it determines specific attainments, were somewhat exaggerated. Few nowadays would subscribe to the statement made in the Spens Report: 'We are informed that, with few exceptions, it is possible at a very early age to predict with some degree of accuracy the ultimate level of a child's intellectual powers.'[1] Particularly in the 1920's it was urged that tests, which claimed to give a good measure of innate intellectual capacity or educability, should be used to stream pupils into homogeneous groups within schools, as well as for selection to more advanced schooling. Now it is true that the correlations between intelligence test scores, and measures of attainment, over short periods are very high (cf. Chapter VI). But they sink with time, and allow of quite marked fluctuations in the abilities of a proportion of pupils. If, for example, junior-school pupils were grouped by ability into 3 streams at the age of 7, we should expect that roughly 10% would require to move up or down a stream every year, and that only about two-thirds would be correctly placed in the same stream throughout a 4-year period. Such fluctuations may be interpreted as arising partly from changes in the child's abilities and adjustment as he grows older, partly from his reactions to changes in the subjects studied, to fresh teachers, and

[1] The Report went on: 'but this is true only of general intelligence and does not hold good in respect of specific aptitudes and interests'; and it recognized that accurate selection of the border-zone group at 11 was impossible, so that there would be a need for numerous transfers at 13.

so forth. Naturally the alterations in the curriculum, methods of instruction and the general organization of the grammar as contrasted with the junior school, or of the University as contrasted with the grammar school, bring about still more marked fluctuations. Hence many not very outstanding pupils seem to 'flower', and others who were initially brighter drop back, in these new educational environments.

In the light of these findings the dangers of streaming are obvious. Children who are relegated to a low stream, to suit their present level of ability, are likely to be taught at a slower pace; whereas the brighter streams, often under the better teachers, are encouraged to proceed more rapidly. Thus initial differences become exacerbated, and those duller children who happen to improve later fall too far behind the higher streams in attainments to be able to catch up, and lose the chance to show their true merits. (In addition, the teacher of a duller group who does note that one or two are making better progress than the rest, is sometimes unwilling to give them up, or to suggest their promotion.) According to Simon, and Daniels (1955), rigid streaming of this kind often occurs in junior schools at 7 or 8, or even earlier in schools where the infant department is attached. Pupils are streamed into those thought likely to pass or fail the 11+ exam, and subsequent readjustments become progressively more difficult. In effect 11+ selection is being pushed back to 7+, and grammar-school entrance is being determined largely by whether pupils make rapid progress in their initial introduction to reading and number work. As was shown in a small-scale investigation by Khan (1955), such early streaming reflects social class much more than it does real ability, since those quicker to read mostly come from middle-class homes.

This stereotyping effect is particularly serious, also, at the secondary stage, where the modern-school curriculum naturally falls more and more behind that of the grammar school. Unpublished research by Vernon has shown that, after three years in the modern school, pupils are more retarded relative to grammar-school pupils than when they entered—not because they have learnt nothing but because, with lesser pressure of examinations, homework, etc., they have not continued to learn as rapidly as have grammar pupils. Not only attainments test scores, but also intelligence quotients, show this tendency to diverge as a result of streaming (Vernon, 1955; Daniels, 1955). Doubts have also been thrown on the wisdom of segregating Educationally Subnormal pupils in special schools for the same reason, namely that many who might improve sufficiently to return to normal schooling later may get stuck at a lower level.

While agreeing with Simon and others that the 'freezing' of abilities through streaming is to be deplored, the situation is in fact far more complicated than they make out. To begin with, the majority of English schools are so small as to have a yearly entry of less than, say, 40 pupils,[1] and in such schools there is unlikely to be any formal streaming. All the pupils in an age-group (or in several age-groups) are normally taken by the same teacher, and even if she subdivides within the class, she can very readily shift pupils from one sub-group to another. Sometimes, on the other hand, the teacher allows this sub-grouping to become at least as rigid as the streamed classes of larger schools. When there are 50 to 100 pupils a year, streaming is very commonly based on some combination of the date of entry of the pupils and their progress; e.g. the duller ones with birth-dates May–August join up with the brighter ones born in September–December; and such classes are frequently regrouped later. Moreover individual promotions or retardations do occur at any stage in most primary schools. Daniels claims to have found that children relegated to C-streams at 7 fall farther and farther behind the A-streams in the ensuing 4 years, in I.Q. as well as in attainments, and that an average divergence of 12 I.Q. points is thereby produced. Now while it is possible that this happens when streaming is very rigid, we doubt whether it is typical. A further study of some 30 schools in a southern county, ranging from 1-stream to 6-stream, was carried out by Blandford (1957). Intelligence and attainments tests had been applied to all pupils at about the age of 8 years. A slight tendency was found for the Standard Deviation, or spread, of intelligence and attainments quotients to be higher at 11+ (in comparison with the 8-year figures) in the

[1] Admittedly the minority of schools with more than a single-form entry may comprise a majority of pupils.

larger, more streamed schools than in the smaller ones. Again the correlation between the 8 and 11 year results was slightly exaggerated in the former. But the apparent extent of divergence of I.Q.s or E.Q.s due to streaming (i.e. the exaggeration of initial differences) amounted only to 1 or 2 points on the average, not to 12 points. This would suggest then that (at least in one county) the majority of large as well as of small primary schools do successfully retain a fair degree of flexibility of organization and promotion. Nevertheless we admittedly have far too little information on desirable and undesirable streaming policies, and how widespread they are. And it is clear that secondary-school selection, which necessitates segregation between schools—as distinct from grouping within schools—does produce more serious stereotyping.

Other Arguments For and Against Streaming. Because the correlations between different attainments tests, or between such tests and intelligence tests, are quite high, educational psychologists have also sometimes assumed that pupils would show much the same capacity in all school subjects. However, Burt showed as early as 1917 that primary-school subjects tend to group into the linguistic, numerical and manual types. Thus success at any one test depends partly on general all-round ability, partly on more specialized linguistic or other abilities. Such differentiation becomes more marked among secondary pupils (who are selected, and therefore relatively homogeneous in general ability), and is commonly allowed for by the system of cross-classification or setting. Yet these general and group factors, as Burt and other psychologists term them, do not by any means tell the whole story. Individual children show marked variations on specific topics, depending on their particular past experiences and interests, also on their emotional reactions to the teacher and to other pupils. Thus if children are satisfactorily streamed for any one topic, the group will almost certainly be heterogeneous for other topics. Current opinion among psychologists is therefore generally more in favour of individual and small-group work within classes, particularly at the primary stage, since this makes for much greater flexibility than the permanent streaming of classes for all subjects.

One of the most obvious difficulties with ability-grouping is that younger and brighter children have to be put in the same group as older duller ones (unless the school is large enough to permit several streams at each age). The latter tend to be bigger physically, and often more mature socially and emotionally (despite the tendency for physical and character qualities to correlate positively with intellectual). Bad feeling is apt to arise, the bright youngsters perhaps becoming conceited, the older dullards depressed and resentful. Indeed the mere fact of being in an A or a D or lower stream creates emotional problems, in the children and in their parents, which cannot be overcome merely by naming the classes differently. All concerned soon get to realize which is the backward and which the advanced class. This difficulty is, of course, aggravated when schools, and not merely classes, are streamed. Terman (1930) has been able to demonstrate that very bright children promoted to classes above their own age do not show any ill-effects later in life. Possibly those who are retarded below their own age-group are more liable to develop a lasting sense of frustration and dislike of education. But we would expect that, when this does occur, it is due much less to the pupil's natural reactions than to attitudes of inferiority engendered by parents or teachers. There seems to be little reliable evidence; though one small-scale study by Rudd (1956) did indicate some personality deterioration among lower streams in a modern school.

Another argument which is sometimes put forward for unstreamed classes is that the duller pupils are stimulated by the presence of brighter ones to do better. This is almost certainly false. In a group of their intellectual equals, where the work is adjusted to their limited capacities, they may be temporarily depressed, but are ultimately likely to make better progress and to be happier. No one who has observed feeble-minded children hopelessly left behind in an ordinary school and then making excellent progress in an E.S.N. school, could continue to doubt that some streaming is advisable.

It is often urged, again, that streaming is undemocratic; that children should learn to mix with all grades. The bright child who is educated only with others of the same level may become intolerant as well as conceited. This situation need not arise where there is streaming within the school, since it is easy to stream for the major intellectual school subjects and to mix all streams thoroughly for social, athletic, artistic and many other school activities. However, it is difficult for psychologists, as such, to comment on a topic which is so closely bound up with social values. As we have already pointed out, some parents approve and others disapprove of their children mixing freely with children of lower and higher intellectual grades, since this usually involves contact with those of lower or higher social class. One point can be made: such little evidence as there is (e.g. Hartshorne and May, 1928) suggests that the school has far less effect in the production of social attitudes than does the home, together with other influences outside school hours.

We see then that there are many arguments against, as well as for, streaming. The crucial questions are—does it really make for greater effectiveness of learning, and does it affect personality development? Neither can be satisfactorily answered owing to the difficulties of setting up clear-cut experimental situations, and of controlling other variables. In respect of achievement, some limited comparisons of schools which do and do not stream have been carried out in America, and these appear to show no appreciable differences. Burt, and other psychologists who favour ability grouping, quote cases of primary schools which obtained far better results in the special place examination when they reorganized their classes on the basis of intelligence tests.[1] Again it is very generally believed that the English system of segregating grammar- and public-school pupils at 11 or 13+ from the mass of average and duller pupils, and putting them into better equipped schools with more highly qualified staff, produces better material for the university than does the American or New Zealand system of the common high school. Yet here also there is no satisfactory scientific evidence. True it is found that British university students usually score higher than their American counterparts on

[1] These occurred at a time when 'The Scholarship' included considerably more advanced scholastic material than is usual nowadays. Few pupils could cope with the type of questions set unless they had been taught in a specially segregated, bright stream.

standardized attainments tests; but this may well be due merely to the much smaller proportion, i.e. the greater degree of selection, of British students. And even if the American system does to some extent retard the top 10% or so, it may do more for the average pupil, and particularly for the 'late developer', who sometimes fails to get the chance he deserves under English conditions. Such arguments from comparative education are also extremely dubious, when the whole set-up and aims of the education systems in the different countries are so different.

The only reasonable conclusion would seem to be a compromise, namely that some grouping by ability is desirable when the range is very wide, but that in general it should be avoided in favour of grouping by age, and should be kept as flexible as possible till a fairly late stage. Up till at least 9 years we see no real case for any streaming, apart from the segregation of the low-grade feeble-minded, and temporary E.S.N. or retarded classes. This does not mean that brighter pupils should not be encouraged to progress more rapidly than the rest, but this should be done by individual assignments or by grouping within the class; and care should be taken to see that such grouping also does not become too stereotyped. However, by the age of, say, 13, the range of ability has become far wider and—in the interests of university studies and professional and technological training—some specialization has to be introduced. Hence streaming by ability and, to a limited though increasing extent by speciality, would seem legitimate. Between these ages we can only urge that such streaming as is imposed by the educational system (including the numbers and sizes of schools available, parental demands, political pressures, etc.) should be so organized as to keep what we have called stereotyping to a minimum. There should be sufficient overlapping between the streams to make transfer up or down an easy matter; and sufficient common activities to break down the barriers between them wherever possible. The kind and level of group in which a pupil ends up at 13 or later should be determined by a process of gradual approximation, according to the principles of educational guidance, rather than by a sudden and irreversible segregation, such as is implicit in current selection at 11+.

Alternative Modes of Secondary School Organization. Obviously there would be many difficulties in reorganizing the English educational system to conform to such an ideal. Can we, however, suggest any modification of the present set-up which would help in psychologically desirable directions? The comprehensive secondary school will, of course, be put forward as one answer. Unfortunately this solution has become so embroiled in political controversy that any comment is liable to arouse suspicion. Nevertheless we would venture to point out, first, that no one, except perhaps a few left-wing enthusiasts, intends to eliminate ability grouping in such schools. Those already established (cf. Pedley, 1955), together with their Scottish near-counterparts, stream mainly by ability on entry, and later to an increasing extent by speciality (linguistic, scientific, commercial, technical, domestic, etc.). At the same time they are undoubtedly of great value in eliminating streaming between schools, and thus getting rid of a competitive 11+ examination and the attendant difficulties described in the next chapter. In theory it should be far easier to transfer pupils up or down, or from one speciality to another; but we doubt (and this is our second point) whether this will work out in practice, unless one or more members of staff are trained in educational and vocational guidance, and have special responsibility for ensuring that every pupil is allocated, and re-allocated when desirable, to the stream that suits him best. We might note incidentally that, if comprehensive schools become general, psychology will have at least as much to contribute to the techniques of diagnosis and guidance within such schools as it has to the more restricted aim of accurate selection.

Thirdly there are the familiar objections that the standards of the brighter pupils are unlikely to be as high as they would in a grammar school, and that schools need to be extremely large to yield reasonable fifth and sixth forms. The difficulty of mere size has been successfully overcome at Coventry by subdividing pupils into houses of about 150 each, each house having a physical existence, and including a cross-section of the whole school (West, 1956). As regards standards it is too early to say. Pedley admits some lowering in the sixth forms, but Lovett (1956) finds about as many pupils from his Holyhead school gaining entry to universities as would be expected in a grammar school of proportionate size. One might anticipate difficulties in building up among the cleverer pupils the intellectual ideals and morale which constitute so important a factor in grammar-school achievement. Yet this is not borne out by Scottish experience, nor, apparently, in Anglesey or Coventry. In general some lowering of efficiency might be expected, just as there is in the most comprehensive of all schools, namely the rural school where two or three teachers cope with pupils of all ages from 5 to 15; also just as there might be if, say, doctors, teachers and bricklayers, etc. all had to be trained in the same polytechnic instead of in separate institutions. Yet even if achievement at the top end was reduced (and this has yet to be proved), it is possible that the level of average and duller pupils would be raised above that current in present-day modern schools.

On psychological grounds, then, there would seem to be more to be said in favour of comprehensive schools than against. But at the same time it would be unwise to ignore the strength of tradition and parental prejudice. As mentioned in Chapter I, these seem likely to frustrate the development of the comprehensive system in any area where segregated grammar, direct-grant or independent schools are available. Thus it would be pointless to recommend their wholesale adoption, or to regard them as the universal panacea for all the problems of selection. But in areas where it would be possible to make a clean break with the traditional organization, they offer a new and promising approach to the difficulties of streaming; and we welcome those already in existence, or planned for the next few years, as providing valuable experience and evidence on which to base future policy.

An alternative type of organization, which has several psychologically desirable features, would be the intermediate school from 11 to 13. The curriculum of such schools would be planned to be diagnostic, i.e. to bring out the educational strengths and weaknesses of the pupils in different directions so that they, and their parents and teachers, would have a much clearer idea at the end of it as to the type of secondary education for which they were best fitted. The numbers desirous of continuing an academic course beyond 13 would probably be greatly reduced, and the secondary schools for 13+ pupils might more readily take on a multi-lateral character. So that though there might still have to be transfer examinations at 13, they could be more allocational than selective in nature; and the greater maturity of the pupils would considerably reduce the strain involved. Obvious disadvantages would be the additional break in every child's school career, the danger of the ablest children being held back unduly, and the shortness of the secondary period left for the majority. Thus experiments along these lines would probably be more feasible if and when the school leaving age is raised to 16.

Another tendency to be welcomed on psychological grounds is exemplified in Southampton, which is developing a much wider variety of secondary schools than merely the grammar type and the modern type. Although we saw earlier that accurate classification along the lines of special abilities and interests is not possible at 11, yet if parents can be offered a choice of half a dozen schools with different vocational biases, and a considerable overlapping in ability ranges, there would be a much better chance of breaking down the competitive selection system, and establishing something like true parity of esteem. Naturally this plan could function only in fair-sized boroughs, but its wider adoption might lead to a considerable modification of the social attitudes that have led to the present impasse.

It is often suggested that raising the grammar-school provision to over 30% in all areas would provide the solution, since the great majority of ambitious parents could then be satisfied. This would seem unwise so long as the grammar schools are devoted almost exclusively to academic studies, and there are insufficient technical schools. Indeed strong arguments have been put forward by W. P. Alexander for reducing their entry to some 5% of the population instead of increasing it. We would agree that some evening-up of the provision in different areas is desirable; but a uniform percentage over the whole country would be quite unjustified. If it were adjusted, either to the existing variations in ability levels in different districts, or to the variations in percentages of early grammar-school leavers (the latter being a useful index of genuine parental demand), it might still be found to vary from something like 10 to 40%. The question of the proportion of the population capable of undergoing an academic secondary course is further discussed in Chapter V.

All such changes in school organization are inevitably slow, hence some system of selection will have to continue in most areas for many years to come. The obvious way to reduce the number of erroneous allocations is to make transfers easier after the age of 11 between different levels and types of school. Most Authorities advocate such transfers, though they vary greatly in their practices, and the numbers transferred amount to little more than 1% over the country as a whole, and range from 0 to about 5% in different areas (cf. Collins, 1954–5). Still smaller numbers of pupils are downgraded on account of failure in the grammar school. By contrast it is shown, in Chapter V, that we would expect at least 5% to have been wrongly allocated to grammar, and 5% to modern schools. Thus the claim that failure at 11+ does not close the door to higher education, since pupils can return to the grammar stream at 12, 13, or even 15, is only partially justified.

One reason why the transfer system breaks down is the stereotyping of modern pupils' abilities, to which attention was drawn above. This difficulty might be reduced if there were more overlapping between the curricula of upper modern and lower grammar-school streams. One would hope, too, that modern schools will come to regard themselves, not as the final phase in the educational careers of mediocre and dull pupils, but rather as the source of guidance for the future. Their organization and curriculum should be planned to discover, not only the few who should rejoin the grammar stream, but also the much larger number who should be encouraged to pursue technical or other forms of further education after leaving. Psychologists could usefully provide a wider range of diagnostic tests over the 12–16 year age range, which would help in revealing unsuspected talent; and the National Foundation has made some start in this.

Other difficulties of transfer schemes must be mentioned. The holding of formal, competitive examinations at 12+ or 13+ is likely to cause further strain and fear of failure, which could be avoided by a more individual approach. Again, the additional break in a child's career, while justified on intellectual grounds, may yet be upsetting to his social adjustment. It has also been pointed out that a more liberal scheme is likely to denude the modern schools of many of their leaders and, when transfer downwards occurs, to give them in exchange the grammar school's unwanted delinquent or maladjusted pupils. Thus we sympathize with those who argue that any case of clear misclassification should be rectified as early as possible in the secondary career, and that thereafter transfers should be avoided until the age of 15. While it is desirable that each case be considered individually, with all its emotional and vocational implications, on the basis of a psychologist's report, the shortage of psychologists in most areas is a difficulty. Moreover we recognize that it is useful to arrange transfers of fairly large numbers at any one time, since then the receiving grammar school can organize a reception class to ease the transition to the full grammar-school curriculum.

In this matter, as in most of the other topics discussed in this chapter, psychologists may be accused of quibbling and refusing to commit themselves to any definite advice. But this is inevitable in a field where there are no clear-cut psychological issues, and where social policy and administrative considerations are involved at every turn. Indeed it is the proper attitude for the rational scientist to adopt until he has had the opportunity of collecting reliable evidence. Nevertheless we can claim to have reached some positive conclusions. We have seen that any policy involving irreversible segregation at 11 years or earlier is psychologically unsound, and therefore that—in so far as public opinion allows—the common or comprehensive school would be preferable, at least up to the age of 13. And that failing this, or failing the diversification of schools which might lead to greater parity of esteem, the selection system should be supplemented by greater freedom of transfer, despite its admitted difficulties.

IV

Effects of Selection

IN DISCUSSING the undesirable effects which 11+ selection often has on the emotional and educational development of children, it is not easy to retain a balanced view. Like rumours in war-time, so stories of severe emotional upsets and of bad teaching practices tend to circulate widely, and to become more and more exaggerated in the telling; and it is scarcely ever possible to obtain factual evidence on how widespread are such incidents. Yet just as rumours were often associated with lowered war-time morale, so these stories tend to discredit both the efforts of education officers and psychologists to carry out selection sensibly and efficiently, and the genuine desire of the great majority of teachers to co-operate while at the same time giving their pupils a worth-while education. On the other hand, it would be foolish to dismiss all the stories as baseless. There *are* abuses, and it *is* the responsibility of administrators, psychologists and teachers to try to eliminate them. Unfortunately the effects either of real or of imaginary abuses are apt to be cumulative; they stimulate parents and teachers to put more and more pressure on the children, and to try even more intensively to circumvent the operation of a fair and accurate selection system. A very real disservice to education is done by the popular articles and the frequent letters published in the daily and weekly press, which describe selection as a nightmare and which lead the public to believe that it is completely untrustworthy and unjust.

The Home. As shown in Chapter I, parents already have strong motives for wanting their children to gain grammar-school places —particularly those in the middle and upper working classes—

and these are reinforced by their confusion and doubts about the fairness of selection. The more far-seeing choose their places of residence in areas where grammar-school provision is high; and there are authenticated stories of some of them seeking to have their children's intelligence tested at 2–4 years in order to gain assurance that they are likely to pass 'the 11+'. Even at the infant-school stage, many parents start badgering the teachers to put their offspring into A streams, and later they demand homework, or criticize any school practices (e.g. projects) which seem to them to reduce the chances of maximum achievement at 11. We have heard of instances of fathers attempting to bribe teachers, by means of expensive Christmas presents. It is probable that pressure on the schools is most marked in areas where the number of grammar-school places is low in relation to the social class and educational aspirations of the parents, and probably much less serious where a third or more of each age-group can be accommodated. It seems to be specially prevalent also in districts where there are local independent or direct-grant schools of high reputation. Thus in junior schools such as those described by Gibson (see below), some children take not only the L.E.A. tests but as many as 3 or 4 other entrance examinations in their last year. The pressure on the schools is likely to be particularly compelling, too, in small villages where the one or two teachers are known personally by all the parents, and thus find it much more difficult to resist them.

Parents, no doubt, vary widely in their self-restraint and long-sightedness. But even if they avoid telling children directly that they have got to work harder in order to pass, there are probably few who do not convey their anxieties indirectly. The sense of strain naturally increases as the examination approaches. Bicycles or other valuable rewards are offered. Relatives and acquaintances send greetings cards wishing children luck on the fateful day; and it is known that very large numbers of candidates wear black cats or other lucky charms. Far too many parents, again, are tempted to supplement the schools' efforts by coaching their children themselves, or by sending them to tutors, e.g. on Saturday mornings. The number of publishers who provide books of specimen test items in English, Arithmetic and intelligence, and of agencies which issue coaching manuals, gives some indication of the demand.[1]

Although, as already stated, it is difficult to determine the real facts, there have been some attempts at impartial investigation. At the London Institute of Education, W. H. King collected detailed replies to a questionnaire from some 30 junior-school teachers personally known to him, who could be trusted to be as candid as possible. Since they were interested in educational research, they were quite possibly somewhat more progressive in views than the average. But although they cannot be considered a representative sample, they do at least provide evidence for contradicting some of the rash and biased generalizations that are often made about junior schools. They were drawn from 7 different L.E.A.s.

The great majority knew of coaching by parents at home or by tutors out of school hours during the 11+ year; and many stated that parents asked for homework to be set. But three-quarters of them denied that parents tend to put pressure on the schools for extra work. When the head teacher was known to be firm, and the parents were satisfied that the staff were doing a good job, there was little or no attempt to interfere with the school syllabus.

Another investigation, aimed specifically at providing some reliable information on extra-mural coaching, was carried out over a two-year period by Gibson (1954). His main data were collected in his own four-stream primary school, situated in a good middle-class suburban area within the Manchester conurbation. In addition he obtained some evidence from the heads of 14 schools in other districts (mainly in the north-west). In his own school he found 43% of children being coached by parents, and 24% by outside tutors, giving an overall percentage of 67. The reports from other schools gave overall figures ranging from nil to 24%, but these may well have been under-estimates, since the heads' inquiries were far less detailed than Gibson's own. However, the wide variations between districts, and schools within a district

[1] One coaching agency advertises regularly in a children's newspaper. Another organization issues an expensive set of gramophone records, similar to those designed to teach foreign languages in the home. Advertisements of a certain breakfast cereal include specimen test questions, and imply that children fed with the cereal will do better.

are apparent. The data suggest that children in the better socio-economic areas are more often coached than those in the poorer areas. In Gibson's school there were clear (and statistically significant) relationships between coaching and parental occupational and educational level. Fifty-one per cent of the children of executive, professional and clerical fathers went to outside tutors, as against 17% of the children of skilled, semi-skilled and unskilled fathers. Since this school is in a 'good' area, with several direct-grant schools of high reputation available to the cleverest children, it may be that the figure of 67% is near the upper limit.

The average hours per child spent on paid coaching were found to be 86 in 1952, and 108 in 1955. The average cost to the parent whose child was coached was £10–11. The paid coaches were all teachers, doing this in their spare time, the majority being men teachers from primary schools. There was some indication that, when homework is set in a school, the amount of outside coaching falls. This needs further investigation, but it is arguable that official homework may reduce parental anxieties to some extent and be less harmful than outside or home coaching. The weight of coaching was more on English and Arithmetic than on intelligence.

Emotional Strain. Gibson states also that there was a higher incidence of nervous traits (nail-biting, enuresis, frequent tears, etc.) among the coached than the uncoached; but his observations were not controlled. Most of King's teachers also mention various symptoms of nervous tension, particularly among girls. Some of them consider that the interview (in areas where it is used) is much more feared than the tests. There are, of course, innumerable stories of emotional breakdown, sickness, disturbed nights, etc., among children around the time of the examination, whose accuracy it is almost impossible to check. However, a few case-studies collected by psychologists are worth quoting, even if they represent exceptional rather than typical instances.[1]

[1] Three of these were submitted by Prof E. A. Peel to the UNESCO Conference on Education and the Mental Health of Children in Europe, 1952 (cf. Wall, 1955). The last one came from members of the British Psychological Society's Committee of Professional Psychologists.

Boy, 9:9—Father a General Medical Practitioner. Stanford-Binet I.Q. 163. Attending private prep. school after transfer from a day private school. Transfer due to father's feeling that boy was not making sufficient progress to be likely to pass 11+ tests. Query: 'Should boy continue at present school and do extra work on the chance that he might make the grade, or should he be transferred to L.E.A. primary school now to soften transition to secondary modern if he failed the tests?' Moray House tests gave: A.Q. 136, E.Q. 133. Both tests at 9:9. Despite all reassurances on the basis of these results, boy worked so hard at school that following official allocation tests and pass for grammar school, boy spent several weeks in bed with nervous breakdown.

Girl, 11:9—Father a dock worker. Allocated to grammar school: I.Q.s 130 and 126; E.Q. 122; A.Q. 139. Query: 'Girl depressed and anxious; truanting, unwilling to return to school; complete lack of interest; no participation in school life; lonely and solitary.' Wechsler I.Q. 123. Rorschach showed extreme depression. Girl felt cut off from her former friends and life. Felt she would have to reject family to make grade in grammar school. No academic interests; and no career ambition which would have enabled her to make the effort. Losing weight. Retiring from all social contacts—even at home. Spent all truancy time huddled over fire at home, neither reading nor speaking. Advised transfer to secondary modern school and short period of psychotherapy. Made rapid recovery. Doing very well in modern school. Taking normal part in school life. No school or home problems since. Follow-up over last two years shows picture maintained favourably. (Note the difficulty of making a correct allocation in the first place, in view of social prejudices involved.)

Child, 10:6—Father grammar-school teacher. Stanford-Binet I.Q. 114. Query: 'Mother pressing father to "do something" about the girl not being allocated to grammar school.' All Moray House quotients in range 95–110. Very poor vocabulary; general verbal poverty; reading interest confined to American-type comic. Pale, thin, anxious; tense and apprehensive; showing great strain; formerly suffered from nephritis, specially advised to avoid strain

—but mother uses this as argument for high potential ability held back by school absences. Actually I.Q. tests of Binet type over-estimate potential owing to favourable scholastic background and parental conversational opportunities.

Our last case, though in many respects unusual and almost theatrical, brings out the importance of a factor which has received surprisingly little investigation, namely children's own conceptions of the 11+ examination and selection. It is likely that they often build up among themselves quite fantastic notions of the nature and aims of selection, which nevertheless considerably affect their adjustment.

Girl, 11—Started sleep-walking shortly before taking the 11+ examination, and said on several occasions that she would kill herself if she did not succeed. Her parents were referred for advice to the Child Guidance Clinic by their doctor. Examination showed her to be a child of good modern school level for her area, but not likely to be considered suitable for transfer to grammar school. Her older sister was already in grammar school, but the parents had poor knowledge of the local 11+ system; thus they knew little of possibilities in the modern schools, or of subsequent transfer system, in spite of a good letter to parents from the Authority. Although there were some indications that parental demands may have been contributing, it was considered that the child's perception of the 11+ situation had been instrumental in producing the symptoms. Immediate treatment included helping the girl and her parents to look on selection in a new way so that a modern school allocation could be accepted and not seen as a disgrace. After several interviews the sleep-walking and threats ceased. The Authority passed on early information about the 11+ result, and when the allocation was announced it was taken without any recurrence of symptoms.

Discussion. While fully admitting the undesirability of imposing emotional strains on 11-year children, it is important to maintain a sense of perspective. Too many child psychologists, in addition to well-intentioned but sentimental laymen, tend to under-estimate children's natural resilience. The normal upbringing of every child inevitably involves many pressures, frustrations and disappointments, and the healthy personality readily surmounts these. The problem, therefore, is one of degree. The taking of examinations at 11 is not absolutely bad, any more than instilling rudimentary table manners into the 3-year-old is necessarily bad.

If the emotional effects were as serious as they are sometimes made out, we should expect many children to develop delinquency or other types of maladjustment, and to be referred to Child Guidance Clinics as a result. Such cases do occur, and their importance should certainly not be minimized, but they are extremely rare. Though no comparative data are available, it is likely that such breakdowns are at least as frequent, and often more serious, at the time of the G.C.E. examinations, or at any similar public examinations in other West European countries (cf. Wall, 1955).

The British Psychological Society's Committee of Professional Psychologists (Mental Health) includes among its members most of the senior educational and child guidance psychologists in the country. They were asked to collect data on the incidence of maladjustment, and of the role of 11+ strain. Records were studied in a number of areas over the last five years. In a school population totalling 212,000 there were 5,705 referrals to Child Guidance Clinics, whose age distribution is shown in the following Table:

Chronol. Age:	5+	6+	7+	8+	9+	10+	11+	12+	13+	14+	15+	16+
Percent. of Referrals:	9·2	8·6	13·0	13·6	13·3	11·3	8·7	7·7	7·1	5·6	6·2	1·7

Clearly there is no sign of any rise at 10–11+, but rather a gradual decrease from the peak ages of 7+ to 9+.

Contributory evidence of another kind comes from Birch's (1955) survey of nail-biting among some 4,000 children aged 5–16+. Nail-biting is often regarded as a symptom of emotional disturbance, though the fact that it occurs among 50% of all children shows that its psychological significance must not be over-stressed. However it does tend to reach a peak in the 12+ age-group, coincident with the average age of onset of puberty. But here too there is no sign of any increase at 10–11, although it is often specifically mentioned by teachers who believe that the approaching examination is causing nervous strain.

The Society's Committee made further inquiries from Medical Officers, and in the opinion of the latter there were no special trends in minor ailments occurring over the 11+ year.

Among the 5,705 referrals to clinics, there were 41 in which the 11+ situation was found, by the psychologist or psychiatrist, to be a factor in the maladjustment. They were distributed as follows:

	Cases in which 11+ Selection featured as a:		
	Major Contribution	*Minor Contribution*	*Total*
Severe, needing treatment, e.g. psychotherapy	5	22	27
Mild, e.g. counselling only	9	5	14
	14	27	41

Assuming an age-group of some 20,000 this means that roughly one child in 500 taking the examination suffers to such an extent that help from the clinic needs to be sought. Naturally there will be many other cases which are either less serious, or which fail to come to the clinic's notice. But we may conclude that there is little evidence to support the notion of widespread and severe mental health effects. The psychologists who were consulted considered that most of the breakdown cases who came to the clinics were caused by other factors, such as gross inadequacies in the family relationships, active in the early years of childhood, and that at most the selection system was likely to contribute to situations already in existence, e.g. that it might constitute a further source of anxiety to a child already rendered prone to anxiety by its earlier constitution and environment. In other words, a small proportion of children who are liable to nervous upset anyhow may be seriously affected by the examination and its preceding strain, but the great majority are not, and in practically no case can it be said to make them 'nervous wrecks'. It should be added that many of the psychologists who arrived at these conclusions are strongly opposed to the selection system, as being liable to interfere with the healthy educational and personality development of children in general; they are certainly not out to excuse it or bolster it up. At the same time they stressed the tentative nature of their findings, and the need for more adequate research.

The School. The reputation of a primary school is largely affected by the success of its pupils at 11+. Thus it is only natural that many teachers should still further increase the strain by devoting all their efforts in the last year or two to cramming those pupils who have a chance of passing, and neglecting school subjects or activities which do not directly contribute to this end. Working for examinations or tests is very liable to have a stultifying effect on progressive educational practices, to discourage experimentation with activity methods, group work and self-expression or creative subjects. In so far as this occurs, many psychologists would claim that it is antithetical to the mental health, and the proper social and emotional growth of children (quite apart from any temporary emotional strains that it may stimulate). To quote Wall (1955): 'Education in Europe regarded as the transmission of a minimum culture is relatively efficient; regarded as a way by which children are prepared emotionally for the enjoyment of a full and happy adult life it still has far to go.' The role of the school should not be 'merely to avoid needless difficulties for its pupils; it has, or should have, a positive and constructive part to play in the healthy mental and emotional development of children'.

Another harmful effect often attributed to the selection system by grammar-school staffs is that the coaching received at the junior school unfits the pupils for sounder methods of study, and deadens their initiative. Though observations such as these are inevitably difficult to check, there can be no doubt of the existence of what is called 'backwash', i.e. the tendency among primary-school teachers to train their pupils for the particular kinds of tests or examinations which are used in selection. The curriculum comes to be based on the tests rather than the tests reflecting the curriculum. For example, when English is tested solely by multiple-choice tests, the junior schools often cease to give the children any grounding in the writing of continuous prose, such as the grammar schools would normally expect of their entrants. Clegg (1953) writes: 'If the Committee was to decide that henceforth they would select for Grammar Schools solely on the child's ability to do long division, this form of calculation would be the main and most serious occupation of certain Junior Schools for the whole of their four-year course, to the detriment of many other activities which ought to be occupying those years.'

A further complaint from the grammar schools is that many pupils of only average ability who have been successfully crammed find the work far beyond them. Either they tag along at the bottom of the C-stream, or develop emotional or delinquent reactions as a compensation.

As to the modern schools, it is generally believed that many children who go there, together with their parents, are disappointed and resentful. The former have been dubbed failures at an impressionable age (and some modern teachers, we fear, are apt to rub this in), with the result that any interest in further educational progress is inhibited. Boredom and rebelliousness are indeed only too rife in some modern and unreorganized schools, though the extent of this poor morale is often exaggerated, e.g. in popular articles in the press; and there is no real evidence that it can be attributed to the after-effects of selection.

Discussion. There are particular difficulties in obtaining reliable information on the extent of coaching in schools and of distortion of the primary-school curriculum. Any attempts to prevent or regulate it, or even discussion of the topic with teachers, often lead to highly emotional defence reactions. This is inevitable, since such action implies an attack on the professional integrity of the teacher. (Similar reactions do, of course, occur among parents, in so far as criticisms of their coaching seem to deny their freedom to do their best for their children.) One might reasonably object to coaching and related practices at school if their sole purpose was to raise the prestige of the school, and its head, by producing 'good results'. But the situation is far more complex than most critics suppose. For it is highly probable that a large proportion of any special preparation for the examination that goes on is done for the best of reasons, namely to ensure the best possible education for the bright pupils. A good teacher is vitally concerned over the progress of his pupils. If he adopts a highly moral and professional outlook and refuses to do any special preparation, then he feels that Tommy Jones and Mary Brown, both of whom are clever children who ought to go to a grammar school, may be pushed out of the list by pupils from the school next door who have been coached for the whole year. He is thus the victim of strong opposing forces, and whichever decision he takes may leave him with feelings of guilt.

What do we actually mean by coaching? It might be defined as special preparation for the 11+ (or other) examination, aimed at the improvement of the child's scores or marks, without having any regard to the educational value of the exercises involved in such preparation. Clearly this is a difficult definition to apply in practice. But we believe that the thoughtful teacher, who has some experience of older as well as of 10–11-year pupils, can be trusted to distinguish between teaching practices which do or do not possess real educational value. From this point of view, all instruction or practice on intelligence tests (which goes beyond familiarizing children with what they are expected to do) probably falls within the realm of undesirable coaching.[1] On the other hand many, though not all, of the exercises designed to improve children's performance in attainments tests may be of value in themselves, and genuinely contribute to the children's education.

Turning now to such factual evidence as we can offer: testing surveys such as those of Vernon (1938), Sutherland (1951) and Vernon *et al.* (1955) strongly suggest that the average pupil does make greater advances in attainments—particularly of the more mechanical kind—during the year before the selection examination than at any other stage in his career; and that, once it is over, he progresses more slowly, or even drops back in some respects and does not regain the same level till several years later.

[1] The topic of coaching on intelligence tests, and of measures to offset it, is discussed in Chapter VI.

However King's questionnaire inquiry brings out the tremendous variations between schools. The majority of his informants deny that 11+ selection has any effect whatever on the education of 9–10-year or younger children, and nearly one-half insist that even in the last year of the junior school they can continue to teach children as they think best, regardless of the examination. They suggest that weaker, perhaps elderly, teachers are the ones most likely to succumb to the '11+ drive'. Admittedly these informants may not be typical of the rank and file of junior-school staffs, but the fact that even a few believe that the syllabus would be quite unaltered if the examination was abolished shows that most of the undesirable teaching practices and the atmosphere of strain can be avoided. We know of many schools where the education is very good, but where there is scarcely any mention of the 11+ tests beforehand. The pupils take them in their stride and, indeed, thoroughly enjoy the day or two of testing as a break in the usual school routine. Because such schools do exist, we are justified in attaching some blame to the teachers in the opposite type of school where the 11+ does produce the kind of educational and emotional disturbances which have become so notorious.

The inadequate preparation for grammar-school work, of which the grammar schools complain, is, of course, another aspect of this problem of undesirable coaching. A satisfactory solution can hardly be expected so long as the pressure on junior schools to get as many pupils as possible through the examination continues. Nevertheless some mitigation would be achieved if selection instruments could be devised which had a good rather than a bad backwash effect. If the English and Arithmetic tests or examinations were of such a nature that training for them improved just those English and Arithmetic capacities that the grammar school looks for, then the difficulty would largely disappear. It is even conceivable that intelligence tests could be devised which would stimulate the schools to develop children's all-round thinking capacities, as distinct from their facility with the 'tricks' of the particular test. Unfortunately, little progress in this direction can be reported so far.

In the modern school, the amount of despondency among

grammar-school rejects has probably also been much exaggerated. The great majority of modern pupils are of average or below average ability, and they are more likely to be relieved than depressed by not having to cope with the grammar-school curriculum, and the heavy homework that it involves, and by being allowed to progress more at their own pace. Recent research indicates that there is considerably more anxiety and worry among pupils who get into grammar schools than among those who do not. According to Bene (1955) and Oppenheim (1956) modern pupils tend to have less critical and friendlier attitudes towards teachers, parents and friends. Russell Davis and Kent (1955) have reported a relationship between the academic ability of children and the attitudes of their parents. The children of over-anxious mothers tend to be above average in verbal ability, whereas children of affectionate and encouraging mothers are more nearly average.

Such findings might seem to confirm the idea that 11+ selection is responsible for engendering nervous strain and mental ill-health. But probably they reflect a more fundamental difference between families, which is closely bound up with social-class mores. Even if there were no 11+ selection, we would have some parents more intellectually ambitious, more demanding on their children—as Allison Davis, Havighurst and Eells (1951) have shown in America. Nevertheless we must agree that selection for secondary schooling, under present conditions, tends to become a focusing point for such anxieties. Indeed the ill-feeling and other emotional effects among parents constitute a more difficult problem than emotional maladjustment among 10–11-year children.

Much can be, and already is being, done by teachers, administrators and psychologists to alleviate this situation. Although, as we have seen, some schools become infected far too readily with the attitude of intense competition, others do manage to win the parents' confidence and to persist in a more sensible approach to the examination. By private interviews and Parent-Teacher Association meetings, they can often be shown the harmful effects of their anxiety on the children and the futility of excessive coaching. It can be pointed out that they can usefully encourage their child's interest in books, writing, drawing and number work throughout his primary-school career, but that this is very different from forcing him to do extra homework or to attend tutorial classes under the threat of failing to get a grammar-school place.

Some analyses have been made of complaints sent to Local Authorities by parents, and these often reveal a considerable lack of knowledge of the objects and procedures of selection, even when the Authority has provided them with printed summaries. In one area, where a deliberate attempt was made to supplement written information with a series of well-planned talks, the volume of complaints was reduced from 16% of the age-group to 1%. At the same time one should not forget the irrational foundations of many parental attitudes. However persuasive the rational arguments employed by teachers, education officers or psychologists, many will remain unconvinced. Long-term relations are probably more important than *ad hoc* campaigns. In other words there is likely to be far less trouble in areas where the administration and the schools are trusted and known to be sympathetic to all reasonable parental requests. Nevertheless it would be worth exploring such propaganda techniques as the film, which might bring home to parents what is involved in educational guidance at all stages of school life, including selection at 11+.

V

The Validity of Selection

IN EARLIER chapters we have criticized the selection system on several grounds. Here we have to assume that the present system will operate in most areas for some time to come, and to ask the fundamental question: How far does it select and reject the right pupils? To what extent are pupils wrongly placed in the grammar and secondary modern school? No easy straightforward answer to these questions is possible since they imply involved technical considerations. The basic method of assessing the validity of selection is as follows. Pupils selected by entry tests or examinations are followed up in their secondary-school years. Then their success in the secondary school is assessed by internal or external examinations, such as the G.C.E., and these follow-up measures of success are correlated with the entry data.

Finding an Adequate Criterion. The main difficulty is to decide upon a criterion of grammar-school success or achievement. What is an adequate measure of a pupil's success in his grammar school? This question must be answered independently of the material used to predict success. It is, therefore, not quite so simply disposed of as Emmett and Wilmut (1952) suggest, that is, by referring to correlation between predictor and criterion, for the latter is a 'measure' of the power of the former. It has to be settled on independent educational and psychological grounds.

The essential problem is whether grammar-school attainments, however and whenever taken, are a sufficient measure of a pupil's gain from grammar-school life. As McClelland put it, a child may profit more from a secondary school than his success in school examinations reveals. It is difficult to devise and measure a broader criterion, including intellectual curiosity, the capacity and desire to exercise judgement and responsibility in real life and the acquisition of good attitudes, tastes and values, and most workers have had to 'make do' with the safer measures of academic attainment, sometimes justifying their limitation on the grounds that success in examinations during and at the end of school life ranks very high in the pupils', parents', teachers' and employers' opinion of what constitutes secondary-school progress. One exception was the suggestion by Happold (cf. James, 1952) who differentiated between pupils who were useful members of the school and those who could merely pass examinations. His criterion involved such qualities as 'staying power' and 'helpfulness and spirit of service'. He claimed that the inclusion of these in the criterion leads to fewer cases of discrepancy, but so far no objective demonstration of these claims has been published. It can be argued also that these qualities constitute something we should expect to be developed in pupils by the school. But against this view there are the obvious differences in character qualities that can be found in the pupils individually of any school, primary and secondary. Probably the real reason for their omission in the criteria used up to date is the difficulty of assessing them. This, however, should spur on research to overcome the problem. There is one last observation that might be made about the value of assessing character qualities. If such qualities are incorporated in the criterion a parallel estimate should be made in the 'battery' or 'team' of predictive instruments. We should be excessively optimistic if we expected that the core of the normal procedure, namely, intelligence, English and Arithmetic, would predict character qualities, even allowing for the persistence factor which shows itself in school attainments.

Most workers use the yearly examination results as a basis for the criterion of grammar-school attainment, though recent work by Clark (1956) has shown that teachers' assessments tend to favour the elder and often quieter pupils in the age-group. The use of a single overall estimate of grammar-school success or suitability can also be criticized as implying a false educational principle. Life in a grammar school is necessarily rich and varied and its aim is to provide something for all its pupils. The variety is lost in a single criterion and a multiple one is obviously preferable. Hence the method described by Peel and Rutter (1951) has advantages in that it enables one to detect the significant components in the pupil's attainments. From what has been said in the previous paragraph the method of multivariate analysis is especially appropriate when the criterion is extended to include character assessments.[1]

School Certificate and G.C.E. results have been used by several workers. This has been criticized, but it is less likely to lead to extravagant claims, for the period between entry and taking the 16-year-old leaving examination is the longest possible for the majority of the pupils. The varied levels of *school* performance in G.C.E. attributable to the different policies of preparation pursued in the schools, will also tend to reduce the correlation; in fact uncorrected internal assessments are likely to lead to higher correlation. Inter-school variations in G.C.E. results may be the most serious obstacle in our attempts to use G.C.E. passes as a measure of the best proportion of pupils to admit to grammar schools. Quite a large proportion of grammar-school pupils, the early leavers, never reach the certificate at all. Also it is very doubtful whether those who take only 2 or 3 subjects can be legitimately compared with those who take 5 or more subjects. Hence it is fortunate that we have evidence from the old School Certificate days[2] to indicate that prediction over 4 and 5 years is almost as high as that over 1 or 2 years. However, G.C.E. is a nationally accepted standard for entry into higher forms, industry, commerce and the professional world and so constitutes an important criterion of achievement.

Other techniques of following up the efficiency of selection, in modern as well as in grammar schools, have been adopted by the National Foundation for Educational Research, and by individual research workers such as Nisbet (1955). Nisbet obtained ratings from the staffs of Scottish senior and junior secondary teachers of the likelihood of their fourth-year pupils obtaining a Leaving

[1] Since it may often be practicable to make these assessments on the basis only of a twofold classification the discriminant function suggests itself as a particularly suitable form of multivariate analysis; (cf. Penfold, 1954).

[2] cf. Rutter (1950): Peel and Rutter (1951): Emmett and Wilmut (1952).

Certificate and was thus able to grade a complete secondary population on a single scale. The National Foundation compensated for the inevitable variations between the standards of different schools in a certain area by scaling their marks against uniform tests of attainment, specially devised and applied to all schools. These techniques, however, are liable to exaggerate the validity correlations, because of the stereotyping effect, referred to in Chapter III. We saw that the average standards of grammar (or senior secondary) and modern (or junior secondary) schools tend to diverge farther apart. Hence any agreement between selection tests and later attainment is higher than it would have been had the modern-school pupils been subjected to the same degree of intellectual stimulation during their secondary-school careers as the grammar pupils.

Internal school marks or assessments seem to provide the most satisfactory criterion, but even here there are difficulties. The first is the stereotyping effect caused by streaming on the basis of entry scores, which will tend to boost the correlations unduly.

Secondly, any one school or class constitutes a selected, and hence more homogeneous, group than the whole population of pupils. It is desirable therefore to correct the correlations obtained from the more homogeneous groups for the effects of selection. These corrections often result in raising 'within-group' coefficients of 0.3 or 0.4, or even smaller, to 'total-group' coefficients of 0.8 or even 0.9. This correction process is apt to strike the layman or the teacher as statistical jugglery, yet it is really quite legitimate. Imagine a somewhat inaccurate weighing machine which makes mistakes of several pounds either way: in a single class whose weights ranged from 5½ to 7 stone, the rank order of weights that it revealed might be seriously in error. And yet the same machine would discriminate with perfect accuracy between fat adults and small babies. Now our selection procedures similarly show quite low correlations with attainment in a grammar-school class. But what we want to know is how correctly they separate the most able 20% or so from the lower 80%. And this is what the corrected coefficients show—namely the correlation of the selection tests with later attainment supposing that the whole age-group had been subjected to uniform teaching in the interval. There is the further justification that corrected coefficients can sometimes be directly checked. For example the correlation between I.Q. and Arithmetic Quotient in the total group of candidates can be calculated, and then re-calculated in selected grammar-school classes. When the latter is corrected for homogeneity it does come very close to the former.

At the same time, there are difficulties in making adequate corrections, and these increase as the selected groups become more and more homogeneous (e.g. if they consist of single classes instead of whole schools), and the size of the corrections correspondingly larger.[1] Thus it is likely that there are imperfections of one kind or another in practically all published studies. And yet the cumulative effect of the numerous investigations of the validity of selection which have been carried out greatly increases our confidence in its efficiency.

Arising out of this discussion some recommendations can be made, even though knowledge of their efficiency must finally depend on the results of further research.

(i) The criterion is best based on internal school examinations and assessments. On the whole examinations are preferable to general impressions of attainment.

(ii) The use of G.C.E. results may lead to a reduction in the apparent correlation between the predicting data and the criterion.

(iii) The criterion should be multiple and not merely an averaged overall estimate, for in this way fuller knowledge of the significant patterns of achievement and personality can be detected. It is the business of grammar schools to discover these patterns and to provide the right education for developing them.

(iv) The criterion of 'success' in the secondary school should

[1] The simple formula which most workers have used is appropriate for correcting the validity of a selection test battery as a whole, but is not appropriate for the component tests of such a battery (e.g. I.Q. alone). Nor should it be applied when selection is partly based on other considerations besides the battery (e.g. record-card material or panel judgements). Richardson (1956) quotes a formula which has rather wider applicability. Further discussions of this complex topic are given by Burt (1943a) and Thorndike (1949). Another point often neglected by follow-up investigators is that any new test or other procedure which is being tried out, but which was not itself taken into account in selection, will tend to show higher validities than will those instruments on which selection was actually based.

be extended to include estimates of personal development as well as intellectual attainments.

(v) Correlations should be corrected for homogeneity, and due regard given to stereotyping or other distorting effects.

(vi) More extended follow-up inquiries over succeeding years, like those being carried out in some counties such as Northumberland, are also desirable for research purposes.

Predictive Power of Selection Examinations. The validity of the objective components of selection examinations and procedures has been the subject of many inquiries. First we may consider the relative validities of the three objective tests in most common use, that is, of the tests of verbal intelligence, Arithmetic and English. McClelland's classic inquiry (1942) showed that standardized objective tests of intelligence and scholastic attainment correlated to about the same extent (0.70) with a criterion of success in the secondary school. (Details are given in Appendix A.)

When we compare these three objective tests we find very convincing evidence in nearly every research of the superiority of the intelligence test as an overall predictor of later success. Thus we have Emmett's results in 1945 which led him to conclude that a standardized intelligence test gives a better indication of grammar-school success three years after entry than the combined ordinary tests of English and Arithmetic. After the war, Rutter (1950) confirmed the predictive power of the intelligence test by correlating it with School Certificate results. In the subsequent research by Peel and Rutter (1951) the test of intelligence was found to be the best single predictor of School Certificate, whether judged from the Arts or Science side. English was a close second as far as Arts subjects were concerned, whilst Arithmetic fell somewhat short in its prediction of mathematical and science subjects. In order to achieve the maximum prediction of a criterion composed of equally weighted School Certificate marks in English Language, English Literature, French and Mathematics, the three entry subjects, Intelligence, English and Arithmetic, had to be weighted respectively 1, ·87 and ·27. The same data from Peel and Rutter showed that the individual correlations between the entry tests and the School Certificate subjects compare closely with the correlations between similar School Certificate subjects. More recent work by Emmett and Wilmut (1952) again confirmed the predictive power of the intelligence test as the best overall predictor of 11 School Certificate subjects. They showed also that Arithmetic was a less efficient predictor of science subjects than English was of Arts subjects (cf. Appendix A). Since, however, other investigators (e.g. Wrigley, 1955) have produced Arithmetic tests which give better predictions of all-round achievement than English tests, the question of their relative efficiency remains open. It does not amount to much either way.

If further convincing evidence of the superiority of the intelligence test is required, we may refer to the comprehensive study carried out recently in the West Riding on the correlation between objective tests at entry and subsequent performance three years later in grammar and modern schools. In the case of 8 out of 12 grammar schools the intelligence test was the best predictor, and its overall superiority was demonstrated by the average figures in both groups. The objective Arithmetic test was superior to the English test when they were compared as predictors of related grammar-school subjects.

So far then as the predictive power of objective tests is concerned, all carefully conducted inquiries show that the misgivings about such material are without much foundation. As a team the three tests most usually employed yield high correlations with later performance in the grammar school. Individually, the intelligence test stands *most* vindicated for it is the best overall test and is the least dispensable. This result is not really surprising, for the testing of verbal intelligence has received more attention from the ablest of workers than anything else in the last 30 years and, in spite of much ill-informed popular criticism, the intelligence test does its job well.

The predictive value of more 'subjective' techniques of selection is fully considered later: 'old-type' unstandardized English and Arithmetic examinations (including the essay) in Chapter VII, and junior school marks and teachers' assessments in Chapter VIII. The general conclusions reached are that 'old-type' examinations, when carefully constructed, can reach the same efficiency as objective attainment tests; and that the essay, despite the unreliability inherent in its marking, does add appreciably to the validity of prediction.

The Overall Validity of Combined Selection Tests. In combination the three objective tests (or intelligence tests plus 'subjective' measures) lead to a still higher degree of predictive efficiency. The correlation of total selection procedures with performance 1 to 5 years later in the grammar school is typically of the order of 0·45, though different studies have yielded figures from 0·60 down to below 0·30. Thus the post-war researches by Peel and Rutter (1951) and Emmett and Wilmut (1952) gave multiple correlations approximating 0·60 with equally-weighted combinations of School Certificate subjects. Within modern schools, owing to their wider range of ability, coefficients are somewhat higher. Such correlations are by no means large; many pupils who enter with the highest selection test results drop to average or below in subsequent years, and others rise. But that is surely to be expected. Children change as they develop, and often react differently to the new or more advanced subjects, and to the new methods of the grammar school. And their work is inevitably affected by their interests and by the social adjustments they make at home and at school, which could not possibly have been predicted at 11 years of age. Much more significant, then, are the corrected coefficients, representing validity over the whole range of ability. Thus in Emmett and Wilmut's research the corrected maximum correlation was 0·86. When teachers' estimates are included as well as objective tests, they customarily approach or even exceed 0·90 (Bosomworth, 1953; Richardson, 1956).[1]

Let us, however, look at the predictions so far discussed in terms of the number of wrongly selected and rejected children. Some psychologists would point out that the forecasting efficiency, even of a correlation of 0·90 is only 69%. However, this index of

[1] The figure of 0·90 may be somewhat over-optimistic for validities over five years. But as Richardson (1956) points out, the reliability of the criterion itself is certainly not perfect, hence it would be entirely justifiable to 'correct for attenuation'. Throughout this Report, therefore, we have assumed that the correlation of an efficiently conducted—though imperfectly reliable—selection procedure with a perfectly reliable scholastic criterion is close to 0·90.

efficiency is based on the probable amount of error in predicting a pupil's actual secondary school or G.C.E. mark. Recent American work suggests that the correlation coefficient itself gives a better index of the 'pay-off' of a selection or classification procedure. However, we think the most appropriate measure of good or bad selection is that which McClelland (1942) adopted, namely the proportion of pupils wrongly accepted for the grammar school and wrongly allocated to modern schools. With a 20% entry rate, a correlation of 0·90 can then be interpreted as follows:

	Successful in work of grammar-school level	*Unsuccessful*	
Passed by selection procedure	15	5	20
Failed by selection procedure	5	75	80
	20	80	100

If we could follow up the performance of all pupils in work of grammar-school level, we should find that 5 out of the 80 modern pupils could have managed it, that is about 6%; and that they would have surpassed one quarter of those admitted to grammar school. The overall errors of the selection procedure amount to 10%.

With different entry proportions, the figures vary. Here are examples where 40% and 10% are admitted, and the validity of the procedure remains the same:

	Successful	*Unsuccessful*	
Selected	33	7	40
Rejected	7	53	60
	40	60	100

	Successful	*Unsuccessful*	
Selected	7	3	10
Rejected	3	87	90
	10	90	100

The smaller the proportion entering the grammar school, the more difficult it is to pick precisely the right pupils.

With a less effective procedure, whose corrected validity reaches only 0·60, the errors (for a 20% admission rate) will be roughly doubled:

	Successful	*Unsuccessful*	
Selected	10	10	20
Rejected	10	70	80
	20	80	100

It will be no surprise to grammar-school teachers to be told that at least one quarter of those selected, on present standards, do not deserve their places. Again it is very much what would be expected in view of the fluctuations of children's work between 11 and 16 years, and it is unlikely that the accuracy of selection can ever be improved much above the figure of 0·90. If the grammar schools are to take in all, or nearly all, the pupils with the greatest intellectual ability, who will eventually be suitable for the universities, they will have to put up with a considerable 'tail' who fall by the wayside.

More public concern is commonly expressed over the wrong rejects—the modern pupils who later turn out to be of grammar-school calibre. Our estimate of 6% needs to be interpreted with caution. Had it been possible to identify these children at 11 years of age and give them grammar-school places, it is certain that a considerable proportion would have tagged along in the grammar-school C-streams or near the bottom of the B-streams; the number reaching 'A' level would be far smaller than 6%. Again it is probable that many of those who shine intellectually in the modern school, and who are regarded as errors of selection because they gain numerous G.C.E. passes, actually do well largely because they are in modern schools. With brighter rivals out of the way they are able to become leaders, and their good social adjustment helps to engender intellectual confidence. Sometimes, too, they get more help and encouragement from the staff than they would have had in the grammar school.

The Size of the Grammar School Group. When we discuss the validity of the 11+ examination, as in earlier sections, we are really concerned with the extent to which the predicting tests place the pupils in the right order of their potentiality to succeed in the secondary school. We may, however, look at the problem in another way by asking not merely whether we have the right order of merit, but also whether we have taken too many or too few from the list for grammar-school places. The usual practice is to take ordinary level G.C.E. results as a measure of the desirable size of the grammar-school group. As in the case of validity this is really an educational problem. What number of G.C.E. passes are we going to accept as an indication that a grammar-school education has not been a waste of time? Several workers have produced evidence on the problem of the size of the grammar-school group and most give their results in terms of the number of G.C.E. candidates obtaining 5, 4 or 3 passes at ordinary level.

In discussing this evidence we should keep in mind the sources of variation in G.C.E. performance between different schools which we have already mentioned briefly. First there are the different minimum standards of entry to the grammar schools on the basis of 11+ examination results. So one grammar school may take pupils down as far only as the level of the mean quotient (standardized intelligence and attainments combined) of 125, whilst another school may accept pupils with a mean quotient of 115 or 110. Many of the pupils who sit G.C.E. from the secondary modern schools have mean 11+ quotients of the order of 100 to 115. Related to this factor is the variation of intellectual quality between different localities, and if the pupils entering the grammar schools are given as a percentage of the total age-group, then this factor enters into the figures. If, however, the grammar-school admission mark is given as a nationally standardized score, then differences due to locality do not vitiate the results. For this purpose it is misleading to give bare percentages, and the minimum admission mark should always be substituted or given as well.

Then there is the variation due to differences of teaching, stimulation, interest and ambition in the grammar schools. So, two grammar schools may draw pupils down to the same level of 11+ quotient, but may produce enormously different G.C.E.

results. This second type of variation is the real problem in research on the follow up of grammar-school pupils to the G.C.E. examination. It is not easy to correct for it, and the uncorrected G.C.E. results will certainly lead to spuriously low correlations with the 11+ examination. Entering also into such inter-school variation is the influence of early leaving. The amount of early leaving varies widely in different parts of the country, even within single Local Authorities, particularly when they include rural and highly industrialized areas, as in the West Riding. Peel and Rutter found that early leavers tended on the whole to have lower mean 11+ Moray House intelligence quotients or standard scores. Lastly, practice varies in grammar schools as to the number of G.C.E. subjects the pupil is allowed to sit; however the minimum objective of most schools seems to be four subjects.

The following material kindly supplied by the West Riding Authority well illustrates two of these sources of variation:

(1) *Grammar Schools A to I*	(2) *No. of Children in the total age-group drawn upon by each school*	(3) *Number and percentage selected*		(4) *Admission mark: Mean 11+ quotients derived from standardized tests of intelligence and attainment*	(5) *Percentage from the age-group who pass G.C.E. in 4 or more subjects*	(6) *Percentage of admitted pupils passing in 4 or more subjects*
		No.	%		%	%
A	321	91	28·3	116	19·0	67
B	863	130	15·1	117	4·9	32
C	721	132	18·2	114	6·1	34
D	462	129	27·9	110	12·1	43
E	204	51	25·0	112	15·7	63
F	394	85	21·6	113	6·6	31
G	108	19	17·6	106	5·6	32
H	462	109	23·6	105	8·7	37
I	103	46	44·7	106	18·4	41

The first source of variation is shown in Col. (4) where the admission mark, given as a mean 11+ quotient, ranges from 117 down to 105. Column (3) illustrates how misleading it is to give merely the percent of the total age-group who are admitted to the grammar school. Such a method fails to reveal that the intellectual quality of children varies in different localities. So, if we compare the areas served by schools A and G, we see that A draws 28·3% of the age-group at a minimum admission mark of 116, whereas G draws down to an admission mark of 106 accounting for only 17·6% of its catchment area. School A presumably draws from an intellectually superior area to the area served by School G.

No table could better illustrate also the difficulties caused by the inter-school variations. The proportion of pupils in each school in each G.C.E. year group who obtain G.C.E. in four or more subjects range from 31% to 67%. But the variation is by no means concomitant with the standard of entry as revealed by the initial admission mark. So in schools B and C with high minimum levels of entry, 117 and 114 respectively, only 32% and 34% of the pupils pass four or more subjects at G.C.E. whereas in schools I and D with lower levels of entry of 106 and 110 respectively, 41% and 43% of their G.C.E. candidates pass in at least four subjects. It is noted also that the four largest G.C.E. groups (in schools A, D, E and I) tend to have the highest proportion of successes (at four or more subjects) whilst the schools with the lowest intakes (B, C and G) tend also to have low proportions of successes. This suggests that uniformity and size of class may be a factor in G.C.E. success.

Material from Northumberland likewise verifies how difficult it is to make use of G.C.E. results owing to inter-school variation. In this county where 13% of the 11+ age-group are admitted to grammar schools and a further 2% at 12 and 13, in one recent year 480 grammar-school pupils took G.C.E., and 360 passed four or more subjects at 'O' level. There was, however, considerable variation between schools. At the one extreme, two schools had a 100% success (four or more subjects) whilst at the other, two schools had not much more than 50% success. Twenty secondary-modern-school pupils sat G.C.E. and not one passed in four or more subjects. None the less the number of modern schools all over the country which are introducing G.C.E. courses with considerable success—Southampton and Bournemouth are often quoted—is indeed striking. Other pupils on leaving enter

Day Release or technical colleges, and likewise attain several G.C.E. passes. And there are many stories of pupils rejected by the normal procedure, who entered private schools or who were later transferred to grammar schools or found places by some unusual route, and who ended up with good university degrees. Both Bosomworth (1953) and Hewitt (1955) find that 12–14 year transfers from modern schools perform as well or better at G.C.E. as many borderline entrants at 11+.

The data produced by Dempster (1955) in Southampton, and unpublished material supplied by Moon (1955), show how well secondary modern schools may do in G.C.E. if conditions are suitable. Some of the latter's figures are listed in this table:

Authority	*% of Modern School places at 11+*	*Total No. of Pupils entered for G.C.E. from Modern Schools*	*Aggregate No. of Subject Entries*	*Aggregate No. of Subject Passes*	*Mean No. of paseses per Pupil*
1	86%	8	31	16	2·0
2	Not known	38	191	102	2·7
3	70%	99	429	229	2·3
4	87%	8	10	7	0·9
5	72%	3	5	5	1·7
6	Not known	6	9	6	1·0
7	Not known	37	165	22	0·3
8	Not known	29	131	47	1·6
9	77%	50	207	98	2·0
10	Not known	5	25	18	3·6
11	Not known	5	30	13	2·6

It is clear from these figures that, on average, each pupil sat some four to five subjects and passed half of them. This is noteworthy since, in two of the Authorities (Nos. 3 and 5), some 30% of the age-group enter selective schools. Moon concludes, tentatively, that there are several children in modern schools in the areas investigated who are capable of profiting from an academically biased education. However the number in any one school is small, and they are seldom able to reach G.C.E. standard in more than a narrow range of subjects. He further carried out an instructive comparison between the performance of a grammar-school group, and of pupils in a selective central school (which took the next 'slice' of able pupils in the same Authority), with the following results:

No. of G.C.E. subjects passed	*No. of pupils passing in Grammar Group*	*No. of pupils passing in Central School Group*
0	3	18
1	7	5
2	3	8
3	6	14
4	1	8
5	2	7
6	4	9
7	0	1
8	2	0
—	—	—
Totals	28	70

The two groups were compared by the t-test and no significant difference found.

Such results are often quoted as showing the whole selection system to be so inaccurate as to be worthless. Our attitude as educational psychologists is, on the contrary, one of surprise at their rarity. Were any other of the older methods of selection employed, there would certainly be far more mistakes. The current methods of selection at 11+ undoubtedly have a higher validity than that of any other large-scale public examination that has been subjected to statistical investigation. Moreover we should remember that a considerable proportion of apparent misallocations represent developmental changes that could hardly have been foreseen however good our techniques of assessment.

According to Dempster (1955), the proportion of modern-school pupils in Southampton obtaining 3 or more G.C.E. passes is about 3%, and over the country as a whole little more than 1%. Doubtless this figure could, and probably will, be improved in the future, though this may be at the cost of neglecting other school subjects in order to concentrate on a few G.C.E. papers, or even at the cost of less care and attention being given to the 95% or so of modern pupils who have no chance of reaching G.C.E. standards. In any case the figure is still much lower than the 6% we might expect, in the light of the imperfect validity of selection, the main reasons being, presumably, that many of the able modern-school pupils and their parents are not keen on the extra year of schooling or the homework involved, and that many modern schools have not the staff or other facilities to push pupils forward as successfully as the grammar schools.

Another line of argument among critics of selection is that the overall proportion of grammar-school pupils getting good G.C.E.s does not seem to have increased since the 1944 Act over the proportion gaining School Certificates and that, despite some improvements, there are still far too many who appear to be unsuited to the grammar school, and who leave early. In one of the Home Counties where the proportion of able children is likely to be very high, and grammar-school provision is nearer 30 than 20%, it is still found that less than one-third of grammar-school entries get 5 or more passes (equivalent to a pre-war School Certificate); about one-third get 1 to 4 passes, and one-third do not reach the Certificate at all. Probably, however, such observations have very little to do with selection. Examining bodies are known to adjust their standards to some extent to the level of candidates entering, and there is no certain information whether G.C.E. successes of the present day are any better or any worse than pre-war School Certificate successes. Likewise the proportion of early leaving depends far more on parental attitudes and the current economic situation than on the accuracy or inaccuracy of selection.

However, the most difficult problem to answer is that posed by variations in G.C.E. successes in different areas, as well as in schools within areas, which seem to bear practically no relation to the proportions receiving grammar-school education. If it were true that roughly one-third of the 40% or so reaching grammar schools in one county do well, and that only one-third of the far more highly selected 10% in another county do equally well, then it would be impossible for psychologists to maintain that low selection test performance indicated unsuitability for advanced secondary education. And at present there are no published statistics to show how far this is *untrue*. Rather more is known of early leavers, and here, it seems, the proportions do increase, though only slowly, as the proportions entering the grammar school increase; (Collins, 1954–5, quotes a correlation of 0·275). Left-wing writers often claim that almost the whole of the adolescent population of Iron Curtain countries successfully attain a full secondary education. But facts are still more difficult to come by.

Some British educationists hold much more cautious views. Robson, for example, on the basis of results in West Bromwich, suggests that we may be wasting our time by going down beyond the top 7% for grammar-school places. A recent Scottish survey, as reported in *The Times Educational Supplement*, concluded that in Scotland: 'at the outside, only 12 to 13% of the normal age-group are fit for a course which is more or less comparable to the English grammar-school course.' Again, Bosomworth claims that, in admitting some 15% of its pupils to grammar school, the Northumberland Authority is making provision for every capable child. However, in the light of our discussion and of the results quoted above, it would hardly seem possible to locate any definite line for dividing those suitable for grammar school from those suited for secondary modern education.

Although the evidence as a whole is far from uniform, the factor which appears to produce most lack of agreement is that of the different standards of teaching, of ambitions and traditions in different grammar schools and secondary modern schools. Wherever the G.C.E. examination has been sat in modern schools, and where a real interest in passing the examination has been shown by staff and pupils, then the results all seem to suggest that we can certainly allow the ablest 25 to 30% of the age-group to sit with every hope of the majority obtaining a reasonable number of passes. At the same time we should recognize that, the farther down the scale G.C.E. courses are extended, the smaller is likely to be the proportion showing the requisite academic interests and ability at academic subjects, and the larger the proportion likely to be frustrated by an unsuitable curriculum.

Can Selection be Improved? In so far as selection procedure is concerned (as distinct from what goes on afterwards in the secondary schools) it might be thought that, by revising the content of selection tests along the lines indicated in later chapters, by introducing junior-school teachers' estimates, and possibly personality tests of the kind described in Chapter IX, the validity of selection procedures could be considerably improved. Actually, when correlations reach the 0·85 to 0·90 range, it is extremely difficult to push them higher by adding further tests or other instruments, however promising they appear to be. But the validities of our present batteries are already approaching the same figures as their reliabilities—i.e. the correlation between any two batteries. The typical reliability for a single objective test, i.e. its correlation with a second parallel test, is 0·95; and by combining the usual three tests, we can obtain an overall figure of 0·98 (cf. Peel, 1948a). Even at this level, 1 in 10 of those passed by the first set of tests (with a 20% pass rate) will fail on the second, and vice versa. But the correlation between two somewhat differently constituted selection procedures is distinctly lower. For example in the Thorne experiment (cf. Chapter VIII), where Moray House tests, National Foundation tests and a procedure based on teachers' estimates plus 'home-made' examinations were applied to the same group of candidates, there were 12% of discrepancies among the pupils selected by the two sets of objective tests, and 17½% of discrepancies between either set of tests and the more subjective procedure. Thus the discrepancies between two different selection procedures are not far off the 25% of discrepancies occurring when any one really thorough procedure is compared with a scholastic follow-up criterion. Clearly we are so near the limit of validity that we can hardly expect that 'tinkering with' the selection procedure (e.g. including essays as well as objective English tests or additional personality estimates) would produce any marked improvements. The particular children accepted will alter appreciably with each modification of procedure, but the proportions of these actually found unsuitable for the grammar or the modern school will change very little.

The implications of such figures for selection have hardly been realized. The size of the border-zone group, that is the group whose selection results do not provide reliable evidence as to whether they will be suitable for grammar school or not, is considerably larger than is usually supposed. Thus Pilliner (1950) estimates it at roughly 7% above and 7% below the actual borderline. But his calculations are based on the numbers of discrepancies to be expected if a second set of Moray House tests was applied. Instead we should consider, either the discrepancies likely to arise when a somewhat different procedure is adopted—correlating little more than 0·90 with the first, or preferably the discrepancies with follow-up performance as indicated by a validity coefficient of only 0·90 or less. We should be ready to admit that an occasional child, say 1 in 100, with an average quotient even as high as 130 may turn out badly in the grammar school; and that an occasional child as low as 95 might come up to grammar-school standard. Thus if we are to be certain of picking up all potential grammar-school successes, we should—strictly—consider practically the whole top half of the junior school population as border-zone. How this is to be done will be further discussed in Chapter IX.

VI

Intelligence Tests

FEW FEATURES of the secondary-school selection examination provoke more criticism and misunderstanding than intelligence tests. According to a *Picture Post* article in 1952: 'Parents are driven out of their wits worrying about their children's capacity to do them.' Particular test questions are often picked out and said to involve specialized information or other qualities—not intelligence; and the absurdity of expecting normal 11-year-olds to do a hundred such questions in three-quarters of an hour is often asserted. Many grammar-school teachers also accuse the tests of picking the 'spiv' or 'slick' type of child, who can answer tricky questions quickly, rather than the really able and persevering child who would make a better scholar. Nor are the tests universally supported even by psychologists. Heim (1954), Zangwill (1950) and others have criticized the mass-testing system, and have drawn attention to what they regard as the dubious theoretical foundations of this type of mental measurement.

Why do intelligence tests seem to arouse more controversy than, say, the objective attainments tests which play at least as large a part in deciding which children will get grammar-school places, and which probably have much more harmful effects on primary-school teaching and on pupils' study habits? It is not because they are any longer so strange and unfamiliar. A very large proportion of parents have done an intelligence test themselves, if they have served in the Army or the other Forces any time from 1942 onwards; and many purchase books of intelligence test items for coaching their children, or at least read the specimen tests which often appear in the popular press. The main reason is likely to be because their children's performance at these tests seems to reflect directly on them. As shown in Chapter II they were first introduced into 'The Scholarship' in the early 20's, largely on the grounds that they measured inborn ability or educability, rather than education received, and therefore gave a fair chance to children handicapped by poor social environment or poor schooling. Intelligence, in other words, suggests something inherited, something permanent, and if a child fails on the intelligence test this cannot be explained away so easily by inefficient teaching, or illness on the day of the exam, or other excuses. Thus parents are much more emotionally involved in their children's I.Q.s than in their performance at attainments tests or ordinary examinations. They are also more upset, and more apt to attack the psychologist, when any imperfections in the tests, such as susceptibility to coaching or practice, are pointed out; though at the same time—irrational as it may seem—they do their best to distort the test results by encouraging coaching at school or by outside tutors, or undertaking it themselves. Intelligence tests are also apt to touch off political prejudices. The strongly conservative dislike them, partly because they are new-fangled, but partly also because they clearly show many lower-class children to be the equal of, or superior to, their own. Communists and many less extreme socialists believe, on the other hand, that they favour the middle and upper classes. The whole concept of inherited ability as determining a child's achievements is rejected in U.S.S.R., and the mental testing movement proscribed.

It is particularly necessary, therefore, to set out the arguments for, and the weaknesses of, intelligence tests rationally and impartially, guided by the evidence of scientific research rather than by traditional theories or by appeals to casual observation, hunches or (so-called) common sense. We shall find that the evidence has led to considerable modifications in the views of contemporary psychologists on the nature of intelligence and its measurements. In many respects the theories given in older psychological text-books, which are commonly accepted both by teachers and by laymen today, will be shown to be inaccurate. First let us describe briefly how and why intelligence tests, as used around the age of 11, are constructed as they are.

Group Tests. A test suitable for application to groups of pupils normally consists of a printed booklet containing a large number of questions which have been shown, by preliminary trials, to range from very easy to very difficult for the children concerned. All questions are 'objective' in the sense that only one right answer is possible, and this is usually effected by the multiple-choice system. Thus instead of asking:

Soot is to black as snow is to .... ?

the correct answer has to be chosen from 4 or 5 alternatives:

ice, wet, *white*, sweep, ball.

Occasionally the correct answer can be delimited without providing multiple choices. For example a Directions Test may contain:

Write the letter which occurs twice in the word SENSITIVE and three times in the word ASSIMILATION.

Again in Abstraction or Letter Series or Number Series Tests, we have this form of item:

1 2 4 7 11 . . . What number comes next?

Items of any one type, such as Analogies, Opposites, Classification, Number Series, Reasoning, etc., may be grouped into separate sub-tests, each of which is preceded by an explanation and sample items, and given with a separate time limit (usually between 3 and 10 minutes). Alternatively, short sets of these items are mixed up in the so-called Omnibus test, and given with a single timing (say 20 to 50 minutes), after some preliminary explanation of all the types. Thus there might be five easy Analogies near the beginning, 5 more difficult ones in the middle, and 5 very difficult at the end. This has the advantage that an untrained tester, using an ordinary watch rather than a stop-watch, can give the test without risk of serious timing errors. In either case the average child is not expected to do more than about half the items correctly; only the brightest and oldest are likely to succeed up to the end. Thus the common criticisms of tests as being too long and too difficult are pointless. Moreover tests are not constructed in this manner with the primary object of setting a premium on speed of work, but rather so as to spread out the scores of the dullest, average and brightest children, and yet—for convenience of administration—to allow all children to finish at the same time.

Such a test must be given under examination conditions, free from distractions; and the tester must adhere to the standard instructions, timing and scoring, otherwise the scores will not be comparable with those obtained from other groups. The test will have been applied previously, under the same conditions, to large and as far as possible representative groups of children, of comparable ages, so that their average scores and range or distributions of scores are known, and these provide the norms or standards for the test. The amount of ingenuity, technical skill and experimental trial that go to the production of a usable test are seldom realized.

Scoring or Evaluation of I.Q.s. There are two distinct methods by which children's scores on such tests may be converted to Intelligence Quotients.

1. A child's score may first be compared with a table showing the average scores for successive age-groups. Suppose his true, or Chronological Age (C.A.) is 11 : 0, and that he scores—not 59 which is the average for representative 11-year-olds—but 48, which is the average for 10 : 0-year-olds. Then his Mental Age (M.A.) is said to be 10, and his I.Q. is:

$$\frac{\text{M.A.}}{\text{C.A.}} \times 100 = \frac{10}{11} \times 100 = 91$$

This traditional method has several drawbacks, though it is useful for children of primary-school age. Beyond about 11 years, scores on most tests do not go on increasing regularly with age. The increases tail off until, after 14, 15 or so, there is little or no further gain. (The precise age varies somewhat for different tests, and different individuals show quite varied patterns of growth and cessation.) The old practice was to allow for this by dividing the M.A.s of persons aged 14 or 15 upwards by a constant figure, say 15, instead of their C.A.s. But this was too rough and ready to give consistent results, and I.Q.s among adolescents were liable to fluctuate for this reason. Another difficulty is that different tests, scored in this manner gave different ranges of I.Q.s. Tests X and Y might yield the same I.Q. of 100 for the average individual, yet the extreme cases might obtain much higher or much lower I.Q.s on Test Y. On Test X only some 2½% of children might gain I.Q.s of 130 upwards and 2½% 70 downwards; whereas on Test Y 10% might score 130+ and 10% 70−. Clearly the I.Q.s on these tests are not comparable (except at the average). Similar variations may occur even on one and the same test at different ages, so that an I.Q. of 125 might be equivalent to an I.Q. of 140 several years later! Although they are quite natural, they are obviously very confusing to psychologists as well as to laymen, who expect a child's I.Q. to be a fairly constant quantity.

2. The alternative method of evaluating a person's test score is by noting where he falls relative to a specified group of similar persons. Thus if he scores higher than 75% of 11-year children in general, he is said to fall at the 75th percentile—i.e. somewhat superior to the average. Similarly a 12-year-old might surpass 90% of 12-year secondary modern pupils, and only 10% of 12-year grammar pupils. His score can then be interpreted in relation to either group. Such percentiles (for a whole age-group) can readily be converted to I.Q.s by means of statistical tables.[1] Thus we know that the 97½ percentile is equivalent to I.Q. 130, the 75th to I.Q. 110 and so on. Strictly it should be termed a 'standard score', since it is in no sense a 'quotient'. However I.Q., like E.Q. and A.Q., is so widely accepted that insistence on correct usage would be merely pedantic. Arrived at in this way, the I.Q. becomes a measure of the person's brightness relative to his own age-group, and it has a constant significance from one test, or one age, to another.

It should be noted that this latter technique of scoring involves an assumption which is sometimes disputed—namely that intelligence (or rather the ability measured by intelligence tests) is 'normally distributed' in the general population. In other words, we are asserting that half the population is of about average intelligence (I.Q. 90 to 110), and that the proportions fall off regularly as we ascend or descend the scale, till barely 1 in 2,000 exceed I.Q. 150. Left-wing writers rebel against the implication that there is, and must always be, a limited proportion of the

[1] That is, tables of the probability integral. An arbitrary standard deviation of 15 is usually assumed.

population with high intelligence. It is true that no conclusive proof that intelligence is so distributed can be adduced, and that the distribution of the scores or the I.Q.s we actually obtain from most tests approximate to the 'normal' type simply because of the manner in which the tests are constructed.[1] Nevertheless, several arguments seem to make it a reasonable assumption.

First: many physical traits, like height, and manual skills, which can be scored in physical units, do tend to yield normal distributions; and there is no indication that tests which involve more mental content begin to alter in this respect. On the other hand, some traits, like weight, do give more skewed or asymmetrical distributions. Possibly the same is true of measures of mental output such as literary or scientific creativity (cf. Burt, 1943b). Secondly: I.Q.s obtained by the Mental Age scoring system do not implicitly assume normality, yet—at least over a fairly wide age range—they do approximate so closely to normality that it is plausible to attribute any irregularities to unevenness in the coverage of the scale (for example, to a lack of sufficient difficult items). Thirdly: common observation suggests that the very bright and the very dull really are relatively rare, and though such evidence is unreliable, it at least does not indicate any other form of distribution as being nearer the truth. It is sometimes claimed that the Soviet system of education produces very different results; but no convincing figures have been published, so far as the writers are aware. Left-wing critics would have had a better case, as we shall see below, had they confined their objections to the notion that no persons, except those who inherit very high intelligence from their parents, can ever get into the top few per cent with high I.Q.s.

Though an overwhelming majority of psychologists accept this 'dogma of normality', we should note that they allow exceptions at the bottom end of the scale. There are more imbeciles, idiots and feeble-minded persons in the population than would be expected (i.e. more than 0·05% with I.Q.s below 50, or $2\frac{1}{2}$% below 70), and it is reasonable to attribute this excess to pathological

[1] As Dr Heim points out, almost any distribution of measurements of human qualities can be converted into, or out of, the normal shape by altering the method of scoring.

causes such as birth injuries and endocrine abnormalities. In assessing these defective levels of intelligence, we are likely to retain the otherwise outmoded Mental Age system. (The system was indeed introduced in the first place for application over the feeble-minded and backward range. Binet never supposed that it would be suitable for superior children and adults also.)

Other Types of Intelligence Test. Group tests are not necessarily composed wholly of verbal questions. Many contain similar items requiring classifying, reasoning, grasping relations, etc., but using non-verbal material, either pictures or abstract diagrams. These are occasionally employed in 11+ selection, but tend to give less useful results (except possibly in predicting scientific and mathematical promise); since the ability needed for grammar-school work is itself so verbally biased. Still other group tests involve verbal problems but no reading of instructions, since they are applied orally. Oral and pictorial tests are more suitable than verbal for younger schoolchildren. For it has been shown that the ordinary 11+ group test requires at least a 9-year level of reading skill. This means that, for the more backward 11-year-olds, the intelligence test becomes largely a test of ability to read the instructions and questions.

Individually administered tests usually follow quite a different type of construction, and incidentally avoid reading difficulties, since almost all the questions are given orally, or by practical demonstration. The original Binet-Simon scale (as revised in 1911) consisted of short sets of intellectual tasks chosen, on the basis of previous trials, as appropriate to the mental level of average 3, 4, 5 . . . 12-year-olds (plus a few for older children and adults). A child does not have to attempt all the items he can manage within a given time, as in the group test. Instead successive sets are applied, ranging from the age level that he can manage completely up to the level where he fails completely. From this, his own level on the Mental Age scale can be calculated. Many translations and more elaborate revisions have been published, the most widely used being Terman's Stanford-Binet scale (1916) and the Terman-Merrill or New Stanford Revision (1937). The latter is still generally employed by British psychologists for the accurate assessment of an individual child, though some favour its replacement by the WISC or Wechsler Intelligence Scale for Children (1949). Any of these are likely to take a skilled tester a half to one hour for each child, hence they cannot be used for testing large numbers. They are definitely unsuitable for application by teachers or others who have not been carefully trained to use them. Nevertheless some L.E.A.s do arrange for a limited number of borderline or doubtful 11+ candidates to be individually tested by a psychologist, before making a decision. And the individual test is always preferred for assessing children who attend a Child Guidance or Educational Clinic, or in recommending transfer to an E.S.N. school. The main reason for its greater trustworthiness is that the tester has more control over the child, can ensure that he is co-operating, that he knows what to do, and is expressing the maximum intelligence of which he is capable. Although experiments show group-test results to be much less affected by keenness, state of health, distractions, etc., than many people might expect, it is none the less true that we cannot control all the relevant circumstances that influence each individual child. For example, failure to follow the instructions, or turning over two pages at once, may be signs of poor intelligence; but they are not the same thing as failure to do the test when fully understood. The facts about coaching and practice, mentioned later, show that children who lack familiarity with the particular group test they are set to do are distinctly handicapped. Moreover there is considerable evidence that a small proportion of maladjusted, anxious or excitable children may fail to do themselves justice on some occasions, and tend to fluctuate more widely from one test to another, than does the more normal child (cf. Connor, 1952). In such cases, the greater flexibility of the individual test is particularly desirable. Yates (1953) likewise reports that a considerable proportion of those children who make exceptionally large I.Q. gains on taking more than one group test do so because their initial scores were depressed by 'lack of incentive, illness, anxiety, emotional disturbance or conflict'.

Another important difference is that the Terman-Merrill testing situation is a much more natural one. The test questions are given without any stress to work quickly, and the child supplies his answers in his own words; he does not select them as with multiple-choice items. The types of items in an individual scale are usually more varied and interesting. Many of them are based on pictorial or practical rather than purely verbal problems. Terman-Merrill is often usefully supplemented by purely practical tests (known as performance tests), based on fitting shapes into holes, constructing patterns, drawing mazes, etc.; and the WISC contains several of these, thus yielding a performance test as well as a verbal test I.Q. Most psychologists therefore regard an individual test I.Q. as giving a more reliable and representative all-round survey of a child's intellectual powers, although there is in fact no evidence that it is more predictive of ability to do grammar-school work than is the result of a group test.

In concluding this section, we would agree with psychologists like Heim who consider that the group test tends to take too mechanical a view of mental measurement. Mental abilities are very different from physical traits like height, which stay the same more or less regardless of the circumstances of measurement. In normal life, people think and behave intelligently or unintelligently in a certain social and emotional context. Just because we happen to be concerned only with the intellectual or cognitive aspect, we cannot ignore all the other relevant factors, such as the child's attitudes. The individual tester can fairly effectively keep such factors constant. The group tester should take more account of them, and investigate more fully how they affect test performance and how they can be controlled. Thus more attention should be paid to the possible effects of children being over-anxious or excited about the test, and whether —for example—they think that as many items as possible must be attempted or whether they are concentrating on accuracy. It may be that testers should not be employed unless they have been trained in instilling the right atmosphere and getting across the instructions properly. At the moment it is only too likely that some teachers commit gross errors of testing technique, such as criticizing or helping children who put down wrong answers, adding to or omitting some of the instructions, mis-timing (particularly of tests given in separate sub-test form), and mis-scoring. Even when the scoring is checked it is quite easy for errors to escape notice. At the same time we must insist that these weaknesses of group tests are nothing like as serious as some critics suppose; otherwise it would be impossible for the I.Q.s to provide as good predictions as they do of future educational ability. Perhaps their most disturbing consequence is, not that they lead to many miscarriages of justice, but that they lead to the wide circulation of exaggerated stories and tend to bring the whole of testing and psychology into disrepute.

What Do Intelligence Tests Measure? Critics who glance at some of the tests in common use, or who are surprised by the low or high scores of children whom they expect to do well or badly, are very apt to question whether the tests really measure intelligence. And their doubts are reinforced when they learn that psychologists have no generally agreed definition of just what it is they are trying to measure. Instead there seem to be a lot of conflicting theories and complicated statistical arguments. Before discussing these problems, we should point out that no one should expect to be able to tell what abilities a test involves merely by looking at it, particularly when the test is constructed for examining children's mentalities. Much better evidence than teachers' subjective impressions is needed for such statements as that I.Q. tests select the 'spiv' type of pupil. Occasional surprising results also are quite unconvincing, since it is only too easy to confuse troublesome behaviour, or lack of industriousness, or poor achievement due to poor schooling or other causes, with lack of intelligence. The main object of introducing intelligence tests was to eliminate such vagaries of human judgement, and to provide an objective assessment of ability. Sometimes one even hears complaints that a thoroughly badly behaved or lazy child has obtained a high I.Q., or that one with outstanding artistic, mechanical or other talents got a mediocre result. These are based on a complete misunderstanding. Intelligence tests would not be serving the functions for which they are designed if they did reflect character or emotional traits, or specialized—as contrasted with general all-round—ability.

Admittedly, however, there are very real difficulties in deciding what sorts of items to include in an intelligence test. Items for a test of, say, mechanical aptitude, can be devised and selected on the quite straightforward grounds that men who are known to be good mechanics do them better than poor mechanics. Again the choice of items for a test of English attainment can be guided by the English syllabus the schools are trying to cover. There is no such external criterion of intelligence, and in its absence, the following have been used:

(*a*) Items show an increase in pass-rate as children grow older. This is a necessary but not sufficient qualification. Arithmetical attainment items, or size of shoes, also increase with age. Moreover it is useless for picking items to test persons brighter than the average 15-year-old.

(*b*) Items are done better by children judged as intelligent by their teachers than by dull ones. This too is useful, but the flaws have been pointed out above.

(*c*) Items appear to the psychologist to involve intelligence. Unfortunately, as already admitted, opinions differ; and even items which are generally acceptable to psychologists may involve other abilities besides intelligence.

(*d*) The results from any one type of item should agree with those of other presumed tests of intelligence. In Moray House and National Foundation tests, for example, preliminary trials will have shown that every item does correspond fairly closely with scores on the test as a whole. When criticisms are raised against particular items because they appear silly, or because alternative answers seem possible, this fact that every item of the test has itself been tested is forgotten.

The obvious objection to (*d*)—at least as the sole criterion of choice—is that it tends to perpetuate or even reinforce any errors or biases. If Binet's original scale, or the early group tests of 1917, were badly conceived, all subsequent tests resembling them are likely to be equally poor measures of intelligence. Indeed new items which might be more indicative of intelligence will tend to be rejected because they do not agree so well with the conventional type. It is a reasonable comment on the 11+ I.Q. tests that, in the interests of high statistical reliability, they may have become unduly narrow or artificial, i.e. less valid measures of intelligence.

Here we must introduce the conceptions of factor analysis, which are fundamental to psychological test construction. Over 50 years ago, Spearman noted that all tests of mental abilities, however varied, tended to overlap or to correlate positively with one another to a greater or lesser extent. Those who were above average in any one ability tended to be above average on all others. This suggested that there was some underlying ability or 'general factor' running through them, and he was able to show (within the limitations of his rather meagre experimental data) that such a common factor could actually account for all the observed correlations. He called this factor '*g*', for *general* ability, but did not explicitly identify it with intelligence because, as he pointed out, there was no satisfactory agreement about the meaning of 'intelligence'. Intelligence is necessarily a subjective theory about the nature of mental faculties, whereas *g* is an empirical fact. As Burt pointed out, it is the Highest Common Factor that can be extracted from analysing any set of test scores. Nevertheless, tests which would be generally regarded as involving 'higher' mental processes (thinking, reasoning, classifying and abstracting, and in particular the grasping of relationships) were in fact found to involve *g* to a much greater extent than tests of sensory or manual capacities, or of more habitual or rote mental functions. Thus the aim of most mental testers (in Britain at least) has been, not to choose quite arbitrarily test items which looked as though they depended on intelligence, nor merely to copy the items which earlier psychologists regarded as involving intelligence, but to find types of items each of which could be shown statistically to be highly dependent on *g*, and by combining these to provide a still more 'saturated' *g* test.

This procedure was logical and scientific. Spearman seemed to have solved the problem of measuring something which could not be precisely defined. But as more data accrued from applying more varied tests to larger numbers, certain flaws became apparent. Spearman considered that the content of any test, in so far as it did not consist of *g*, was something completely specific to that test alone. Any set of tests should measure the same *g*, as no other common factor existed; though he admitted a few exceptions, i.e. sub-types of ability such as the mechanical and the musical.

Burt, on the other hand, provided evidence of numerous 'group factors', or sub-types of ability present in groups of similar tests. While Thurstone and his followers in America went almost to the other extreme, and—using more flexible factor-analytic techniques than those of Spearman—classified the mind's abilities into a whole series of more or less distinct factors: verbal reasoning, fluency, rote memory, number, spatial, and many others. For them *g*, if it appeared at all, was secondary to these group factors (cf. Vernon, 1950). Teachers and laymen, and even many psychologists, find it difficult to see the value of factor analysis when such apparently complete disagreement reigns between the views and the findings of experts like Spearman, Burt and Thurstone. Actually the differences are relatively minor nowadays; mental traits and abilities can be classified in many different, yet plausible ways, much as human bodies, for example, might be classified primarily by the general dimension of size, or else by numerous more detailed characteristics of particular limbs. The important point is that both British and American factorists now agree that different mental tests, with varied form and content, do measure somewhat different factors over and above *g* and their separate *s*'s or specific elements. For example, verbal group tests do embody an important verbal component or *v* factor, which is not present in most non-verbal group or individual performance tests. Though less clearly proven, it is likely that such tests, based on multiple-choice items done at speed, likewise measure a factor (or factors) of ability at this kind of material, which is absent from the Terman-Merrill test. It is the presence of such additional factors, which have little or no relevance to successful school work or to manifestations of intelligence in everyday life, that is largely responsible for the artificiality and lowered validity of verbal group tests, already referred to. At the same time this defect should not be exaggerated, since for the most part these tests do measure the same *g* and *v* as Terman-Merrill, or indeed as any improved intelligence test likely to be designed in the future; and these factors are extremely relevant to grammar-school success.

It can be seen then that the foundations of Spearman's views are undermined, and that we still have no objective criterion for assessing whether or not a test is really a test of intelligence. And yet the present position is much less unsatisfactory than it sounds, for the following reasons. Although factor analysis does not enable us to pin down the essence of intelligence or the nature of the central factor, it has developed to the stage where it can very effectively analyse and classify the component abilities in a number of tests. For instance, it can determine whether 'facility-at-doing-multiple-choice-items' is an important element in any test; or whether some mental function—say judgement or common sense or creativeness—which we might wish to include in our concept of intelligence, is excluded by our present tests, and so forth. Moreover there has emerged in recent psychological writings, such as those of Hebb and Piaget, a more consistent theory of intellectual development. We realize that intelligence is not any one definite faculty or power of the mind. It includes all the mental functions which have been mentioned in the apparently conflicting definitions given in the past, and indeed permeates all our behaviour and thinking. Our tests can emphasize any group factors, i.e. any aspects of intelligence, that we wish. Thus most of our present group tests are mainly tests of 'academic aptitude'. They emphasize capacity for dealing with complex concepts, for comprehending or grasping relations, for abstract reasoning and new verbal learning. Individual tests, though overlapping very largely, probably give a better sampling of intelligent behaviour in everyday life. Instead of trying to measure some one thing called intelligence, it would be more sensible to choose types of test which give us the best predictions of whatever kind of ability we are interested in, e.g. intelligence for grammar-school work. This means that more careful study is needed of the development of intellectual powers in the course of secondary and university education. On this basis we could devise somewhat improved tests, or purify our present ones of undesirable features, and so arrive at more accurate prognostication of those qualities of mind that contribute to successful grammar-school or university work, which are not already covered by attainments tests and conventional examinations.

Our present tests are extremely useful; indeed it is shown in Chapter V that they are usually our best single instrument. But they could probably be better still if, for example, they gave less scope for slapdash guessing, and depended less on picking the right answer at speed. There may well be some truth in current criticisms by grammar-school teachers, even though they are exaggerated. Such teachers would by no means appreciate having all 'plodders', if that were possible. The real weaknesses in these arguments are, first, that children are very rarely consistently 'slick' or 'plodding'; their attitude to a job varies greatly with the particular job; and secondly that mental quickness is by no means distinct from or opposed to mental power. On the whole those who can think quickly are usually better able to think successfully. Spearman's work has fully demonstrated this point although, as we have admitted, later factorial investigations do indicate that a partial distinction can be made, i.e. that we would get slightly different results if our tests concentrated more on 'power', less on 'speed'.

The same answer can be given to those who think the tests fail to cover creativity and originality, or good memory or a number of other qualities of mind; namely that, to a very large extent these qualities do 'boil down to' the same *g* and *v* that the tests already measure; yet at the same time it would be possible to give them a little more weight. If psychologists seem slow to accept and act on these criticisms, one should point out that the research involved in, (*a*) studying the reality of such qualities, (*b*) devising effective tests of them, (*c*) trying them out and following up children over several years to see if they actually help in selection, is exceedingly elaborate, expensive and time-consuming. Educational psychologists are generally too busy with routine jobs to undertake such work. Moreover teachers and administrators often resent the 'waste' of pupils' time involved in the necessary experiments. Thus progress is inevitably slow. Yet we can admit that the group intelligence test has become somewhat unenterprising and stereotyped (partly because administrators like to be able to rely on a standard product which is comparable from one year to the next), and that they might benefit from a complete overhaul.

How Far Do Intelligence Tests Measure Inborn Ability? As pointed out in our opening, this question underlies much of the controversy and criticism to which the tests give rise. It should be mentioned first that, even if the I.Q. was completely innately determined and dependent on inherited genes, it would still not be true that children must have the same intelligence as their parents. Just as a tabby cat has kittens of a variety of colours, and just as tall parents often have children who grow up to be smaller—or even taller—than themselves, so we should expect some resemblance but also considerable variations between parental and offspring intelligence. Likewise two children in the same family do tend to have fairly similar intelligence, yet often differ quite widely from one another (unless they are identical twins). Such variations are attributable to the varied 'reshufflings' of the parental genes at each birth; thus they are just as much innately determined as are resemblances. Indeed they provide one of the main arguments for an innate component in the I.Q. For children in the same family are usually brought up pretty much alike; and if their intelligence was purely dependent on upbringing it would be inconceivable that they should often show such wide differences. The same applies to children in an orphanage. Despite their highly standardized environment and education, different orphans in the same institution continue to show a wide range of I.Q.s.

Now we must turn to the evidence that environment does affect the child's or adult's intelligence. Quite early in the history of mental testing it was observed that children of gipsies, tinkers or canal boatmen, who received scarcely any schooling, obtained very low I.Q.s on the Binet-Simon scale. This was interpreted to mean that the tests measured inborn ability only when children had had normal educational opportunities. Also it was generally supposed that this limitation applied mainly, or solely, to tests with verbal content. Hence more accurate results could be obtained with non-verbal (pictorial, abstract diagram, or performance) tests. However, much additional evidence has accumulated showing the inadequacy of these views. Studies of foster children by such cautious American psychologists as Freeman and Burks indicated that good or poor foster homes might make a difference of 10, or at most 20, points of I.Q. Expressed in another way: foster children showed considerably less resemblance in intelligence to their true parents than did children in normal families, and showed just about as close resemblance to their foster parents. More exaggerated claims were made, around 1938, by the Iowa investigators, Wellman, Skeels and others, on the basis of studies of orphans and adopted children. They went so far as to say that adopting parents need take no account of the heredity of children they propose to adopt. But their findings have been widely criticized, and in this country Lawrence (1931) was able to show a small but appreciable correlation between the I.Q.s of illegitimate orphans, separated from parents before the age of 6 months, and the social class of their fathers who had nothing to do with their upbringing. A number of left-wing writers, backed by the scientific investigations of Eells, Davis, and Havighurst (1951) at Chicago, have claimed that intelligence test results largely or mainly reflect social class differences. For it is regularly found that the I.Q.s of children of professional parents average around 115, and that there is a regular decline with socio-economic grade down to an average of around 93 in children of unskilled labourers. But Lawrence's evidence, just cited, proves beyond doubt that to some extent such social class differences are genuine, innate ones; that middle-class children do not do better than working-class *merely* because they receive more favourable upbringing which helps them with the tests.

Further important studies have been made of identical twins brought up in different environments, by Newman, Freeman and Holzinger (1937). These too showed that in very different environments twins—with the same hereditary equipment—might differ by as much as 20 points in I.Q. Anthropological investigations are relevant too: it has become clear from work in primitive societies that no test material is culturally 'neutral', i.e. entirely unaffected by upbringing. For example performance tests certainly do not yield fair comparisons between African, or aboriginal Australian, and British children. The latter have far more experience in handling blocks, interpreting pictures, etc., than the former. Moreover the attitudes of different people towards the test situation make a considerable difference. The natural reaction of aborigines to a difficult problem is not to try to solve it as quickly as possible by individual effort, but rather group discussion. Even as near home as the outer Hebrides it has been found that the ordinary group test (translated into Gaelic)[1] does not work, since children there have quite a different tempo of existence, and cannot be made to understand the need to work at speed (cf. Smith, 1948).

If environmental effects are considerable, we would expect frequent changes in I.Q. on retesting, and these do in fact occur. It has been far too widely supposed that a single testing yields an I.Q. which would be constant for life. The pioneers of mental testing like Burt and Terman did indeed point out that test results were not perfectly reliable, and that changes of the order of 5 or even 10 points were quite common. But this prediction was based on retesting after quite short intervals with very thorough tests like the Stanford-Binet. Over longer periods, and especially where different group tests are applied, fluctuations may be much greater. It is therefore unfortunate that educators have been allowed to gain a somewhat exaggerated notion of the degree of stability of the I.Q.

The technical evidence is reviewed in Appendix B. From about 6 to 11 years, the I.Q. obtained from a good individual test is unlikely to alter by more than about 7 points on the average (or, if the child is frequently retested, by 10 points). That is, he does tend to stay in the same band or region. Many children are less variable than this, but a few show much larger fluctuations. Some 17% may alter 15 points up or down, and rare cases may even change 30 to 40 points. Much the same holds when a thorough group test given at 11 is compared with similar (not identical) group tests up to 15 or 18 years. It is difficult to generalize since much depends on the shortness of the time interval, the similarity of the tests, the accuracy of their norms and other technical considerations. But one can definitely conclude that the I.Q. is sufficiently stable to make possible useful predictions in the majority of cases over the period of primary or of secondary schooling. Yet it is also likely to fluctuate so widely in a minority that rigid segregation or streaming by I.Q. would be quite unjustified. It would be still more hazardous to predict from 6 years

[1] In some largely Welsh-speaking areas the intelligence test has to be omitted from selection, not because it is inappropriate, but because few standardized tests in the Welsh language are at present available.

to 18, and tests given before the age of 6 are much less indicative. Indeed the various tests of developmental level sometimes applied to babies from 0 to 2½ provide practically no indication of later intelligence, except perhaps in cases of severe mental defect.

Now by no means all these changes can be ascribed to good or poor environment. There are many other factors which render any single test result incompletely trustworthy, and it is safer to accept the figures already quoted of 10, up to 20 in exceptional cases, as an estimate of the magnitude of environmental differences. This is borne out by investigations into the effects of different types and amounts of secondary schooling. We now know that it is not true (as some older psychology text-books state) that growth in intelligence reaches its maximum at 14 to 16, and that only acquired information or occupational skills continue to improve thereafter. People possessing the same intelligence level at 9 years have been retested as adults, and it has been found that those who received full secondary and university education were now 12 I.Q. points ahead of those who left at 14 or 15 and received no further education (cf. Husen, 1950; Vernon, 1955). This does not mean that *all* grammar schools improve the intelligence of *all* pupils; as always there are large differences, and some grammar pupils fail to get as much stimulus as other adolescents do in modern schools and Further Education classes. Nevertheless the generally better education in grammar schools does usually produce marked effects on test scores; and it is clear that intellectually stimulating jobs and cultural interests favour intellectual development more than do jobs and leisure pursuits which involve very little 'exercise' of the person's 'brains'. The reason why the average curve of growth on an intelligence test appears to reach a maximum at about 15, to stay constant, and then to decline from about 20 onwards is that it hides the differences between the privileged minority who continue to develop well beyond 15, and the majority who get little or no intellectual stimulation beyond this age. (A further point is that our conventional intelligence tests provide a much less comprehensive coverage of adult than they do of childhood ability. Adults express their intellectual powers less in the abstract reasoning and grasping relationships to which we have referred than in specialized professional and trade skills, executive and personal relationships, and in the sort of faculties that we describe as wisdom, judgement, creativity, etc.)

The normal growth of a child's intelligence is affected not only by intellectual factors in his environment. There is considerable evidence that emotional factors are very relevant also, and that intelligence is lowered by many forms of maladjustment, anxiety and emotional inhibition; whereas it is favoured when the home and the social environment generally succeed in producing an harmonious, balanced personality. This is likely to be particularly important in the pre-school years; but older children too sometimes show remarkable rises of I.Q. after attending child-guidance clinics for treatment. A well-known research in America by Schmidt (1946) claimed to bring about rises averaging more than 30 points among children classified as feeble-minded, who were sent to a school where special attention was given to their emotional and social adjustment as well as to their intellectual and manual training. Many psychologists are dubious of the authenticity of this claim. But genuine, if much smaller, gains have been demonstrated by Clarke (1954) among feeble-minded British youths with bad emotional backgrounds, after a year or so in an occupational training centre. Under ordinary circumstances, defectives who spend several years in institutions or E.S.N. schools tend on the average to decline in I.Q. But there are always some who make quite large gains, so that here too it is psychologically unsound to classify rigidly. Many children with I.Q.s in, say, the 50 to 70 range may show themselves capable later of coping with education in the ordinary school, or may obtain regular employment as adults and become self-supporting.

Theories of the Nature of Intelligence. So much for the facts. To what psychological theory of intelligence do they point? A very clear (though highly technical) formulation is given by D. O. Hebb in his book, *The Organization of Behavior* (1949), and this is broadly accepted by most contemporary psychologists. He shows that it is helpful to distinguish two quite different meanings of the word intelligence—Intelligence A and Intelligence B. Intelligence A is innate potentiality or endowment, some quality of the nervous system ultimately determined by the genes, which makes possible the development of human perception, memory, thinking and other functions. We cannot directly observe or measure this, and are unlikely to be able to do so, though we can infer its existence from the facts of inheritance already outlined. On the basis of this potentiality the baby, the older child and the adult build up, first the simple, then the more complex mental processes through interaction with the environment. These acquired capacities constitute Intelligence B—the intelligence that we observe in everyday life, and which our tests represent more or less effectively. In the absence of adequate environmental stimulation at appropriate ages, certain mental capacities may fail to form properly, and the person's ultimate level is impaired. Hebb has carried out experiments with rats and dogs, where some of the animals were reared in the very restricted environment of a cage, but others were brought up as pets in a much richer environment which they could explore freely, and thus experience more varied stimulation. As adults the latter were found to be capable of much better problem solving and new learning than the former. They had learned to be more intelligent. Similarly in humans, Intelligence B is the product of both potentiality and upbringing.

On this view there is no hard and fast distinction between intelligence and educational attainments or acquired information —though this distinction has bulked largely in older psychological text-books. Actually there is always a very close correspondence between intelligence test scores and all-round educational standing (though less close with marks in any particular subject). However, a proportion of children do score relatively higher on one than on the other, and a relative distinction is still useful. By attainments we mean those concepts and educational skills which are specifically taught in school or in books, whose absorption and retention also depends largely on the person's interest in these fields of knowledge and on his personality traits such as industriousness. Whereas by intelligence we mean more general qualities of comprehending, reasoning and judging, as manifested at school or in daily life, which have been picked up without much specific instruction. These do not develop without intellectual stimulation and exercise, but at the same time they cannot be taught merely by drill. Both aspects of ability are worth testing at the 11+ examination, not because I.Q. tests measure innate ability, but because they give more weight to this general level of intellectual functioning, whereas attainments tests and examinations (though agreeing fairly closely with I.Q.) give relatively more weight to specialized training and industriousness. At the same time we should reject the view that Intelligence B 'causes' or 'makes possible' attainments; it would be equally true to say that it is the result of attainments.

We must also reject the notion that intelligence can be taught. It has been shown above that the I.Q. does possess a considerable degree of stability, and although type and amount of schooling clearly have some effects, there is no simple recipe that can be offered to teachers who want to raise their pupils' intelligence. Indeed it is only too clear that many dull children remain in the dull category however devoted and thorough the teacher's efforts. The reason for this is partly that the dull child started with a poor endowment of brain power (Intelligence A); but also that intellectual growth is essentially cumulative. The level of concept development and thinking shown by a child on entry to a primary school represents the product of this endowment and previous upbringing; and these largely determine his capacity for further intellectual growth. Improved education or improvements in personality adjustment may alter his educability, but do so to a marked extent only in exceptional cases. Similarly on entry to secondary schooling, the I.Q. tests do give a fair indication of capacity for acquiring advanced education, not because this capacity is truly inborn, but because it has become more or less stabilized in the previous 11 years. It further follows from our view of intelligence that the tests work all the better in that they reflect environment as well as heredity. If it ever did become possible to devise pure measures of Intelligence A, they would not give as good predictions of future educational and vocational success.

I.Q. and Social Class. For similar reasons, the complaint of left-wing writers that intelligence tests reflect class differences is irrelevant. Most of the abilities we wish the tests to predict are also affected by social class. However this is a complicated issue, which must be disentangled carefully. We know first (as pointed out earlier) that class differences in average test performance are to some extent innate. Secondly, we can be sure that middle-class homes do in general provide better stimulation of the kind that fosters intellectual development than do poorer, often overcrowded, lower working-class homes. But thirdly, within any one class there exists a wide range of intellectual differences, and there is tremendous overlapping between classes. Hence, in so far as children are selected by I.Q., many working-class children score above the borderline for grammar-school entrance. Indeed, because the professional and managerial classes are relatively small, whereas the clerical and skilled trade classes are much larger, the latter actually supply a greater total number of high I.Q. children than do the former, as illustrated by the following figures.

Grade of Father	(*1*) *Percentage of all children whose fathers fall in these grades*	(*2*) *Percentage of all children with I.Q.s of 113+ (i.e. in the brightest 20%)*	(*3*) *Percentage of children in each grade with I.Q.s 113+ (i.e. 20% of Col. 2/Col. 1)*
Professional	2·1	7·0	66
Large employers	1·2	2·7	46
Other Salaried	3·5	8·0	45
Small employers	5·0	8·0	32
Clerical and other non-manual	8·4	13·5	32
Skilled manual	36·0	35·1	19
Farmers	2·1	1·9	18
Semi-skilled manual	14·2	9·2	13
Agricultural labourers	6·5	4·0	12
Unskilled manual and labourers	21·0	10·6	10
	100·0	100·0	Average 20

Socio-Economic Grade and Success on Moray House Intelligence Tests (based on results quoted by the Scottish Council for Research in Education, 1953).

This Table may be abbreviated by combining the first five grades as 'white-collar' and the remaining five as 'manual workers', who represent respectively 20% and 80% of the parental population (Col. 1). Thirty-nine per cent of children of white-collar parents score I.Q.s of 113+, i.e. above the grammar-school borderline, and 15% of children of manual parents (Col. 3). Nevertheless, if selection were based solely on I.Q., 61% of the grammar-school population would come from the manual class and 39% from the white-collar class (Col. 2).

Fourthly, class seems to have a greater affect on attainments, examination marks and teachers' estimates than it does on intelligence. Thus the net result of using intelligence tests in selection is that they operate much more as a class-leveller than as a class-perpetuator; and it would be more logical for left-wing critics to welcome them rather than decry them. In areas where the intelligence test has been abandoned, it is likely that fewer working-class children are gaining grammar-school places than in those where they still constitute part of the examination.

Just as tests help to even out class differences and to produce greater social mobility, so too they are useful in reducing school differences. Although they do not measure innate ability, they continue to serve the function for which they were first introduced, that of giving a better chance to children from small or inefficient schools, or to children who have missed a good deal of schooling through ill-health, etc., and who are therefore below standard in attainments. Not infrequently, for example, children from private schools do relatively better on intelligence than attainments tests, not because private-school education is inefficient, but because it may not have bothered to train the children in the mechanical English and Arithmetic skills which largely comprise the attainments tests. Indeed such schools may sometimes have done more to develop the higher intellectual powers of their pupils, and to make them suitable grammar-school material.

Effects on Tests of Coaching and Practice. A further puzzling feature of intelligence tests, which we have not yet considered, is their susceptibility to the effects of practice or coaching. By practice we imply, taking other similar tests previously (not identical ones, since the actual test used in an 11+ examination is always kept strictly confidential). Pupils are not told the answers, but they do, on the average, show appreciable increases as a result of the familiarity they gain with the make-up of the test, and the kinds of instructions and items it contains. Coaching implies that they are told the right answers to specimen items, shown how they work, and given additional hints on tackling such items quickly and effectively.

It has been known almost since group testing started that such previous experience had an effect on scores. But this hardly mattered when tests were used for educational guidance purposes, or for experimental researches, where there was no particular incentive for doing as well as possible. But when they began to be applied competitively, teachers and parents soon tried to beat the examiners, and to do their best for the children, just as with any other form of examination. For some time, both psychologists and administrators tried to discourage it, and to minimize its effects. Hence there was a certain shock among teachers and the public when Vernon (1952) pointed out that the improvements brought about by coaching were large enough to make a considerable difference to children near the selection borderline. Less notice was taken of his qualifications; namely that such rises were definitely limited, and that they were achieved as a result of quite small amounts of practice and coaching—in other words that they were of quite a different order from improvements in educational attainments which one expects to be roughly proportional to the amount of effort devoted. Generalizing from a number of investigations, Vernon estimated the average rise after a single practice test at about 5 I.Q. points, that further practice brings progressively smaller increases, totalling about 10 points, and that scores tend to fluctuate irregularly or even to drop after 5 or 6 practice tests. Coaching could make a total difference of 12 to 15 points, but its maximum effectiveness seemed to be reached in 2–3 hours. Further confusion arose because other psychologists observed considerably smaller effects—for example maximum average rises of only 6 points—and some even found that uninstructed practice was more effective than coaching.[1] However, these discrepancies

[1] Cf. symposium, *British Journal of Educational Psychology*, 1953–4, 23, 24.

have been satisfactorily explained. They arise partly because the pupils tested have been sophisticated to varying degrees before taking the tests, and partly because the type of coaching differed. Coaching by parents or teachers from published books of intelligence test items, or from other, more or less dissimilar, tests, is singularly ineffective, particularly when it does not include doing a complete parallel test under timed examination conditions. Moreover some teachers are poorer at coaching than others. Though pupils do to some extent become adapted or sophisticated to doing tests in general, most of the effects of practice and coaching seem to be highly specific; that is, even a slight difference in the type of test or conditions of testing may render them almost useless.

Clearly these effects are very different from the effects of environment and education on intelligence in general. Children can be drilled quite quickly into a certain facility at doing particular kinds of test, but there is no reason whatever to suppose that this raises their all-round intellectual level of thinking, learning or behaving. In so far as a good education by good teachers can genuinely increase intelligence, the corresponding rise in I.Q. is to be welcomed. But mere coaching in how to do tests is educationally worthless, and it seriously complicates the selector's problems. In some areas almost all children gain a reasonable familiarity with tests at school. This not only helps to put them all on a par, but also has the positive value of robbing the crucial 11+ test of some of its terrors. Those who get extra coaching at home or from private tutors probably gain no additional advantage.[1] Indeed they may even do worse, either because the coaching is of the ineffective variety, or because it increases the strain and anxiety among these children. Yet there will always be a few candidates, e.g. from private schools, or from schools where the staff refuse to debase their education by coaching, who will be

[1] Such tutors are apt to quote the number of successful examinees who have passed through their hands, and to imply that no child is likely to pass without their aid. But, as shown in Chapter IV, they are mostly employed by middle-class parents who can afford their fees, and whose children have a very much better than average chance of passing anyhow. There is no evidence at all that their clients do better than other children of the same cultural background.

unfairly handicapped if their abilities fall near the borderline. Several authorities have therefore authorized a limited amount of practice and coaching in all schools concerned. Even if this is insufficient to bring about the maximum possible gains among all pupils, it does at least help to bring the previously uncoached fairly close to the level of those who have been intensively and illegally coached, in or out of school. Note that the fact of an all-round rise, even of 10%, in the average I.Q. does not upset the selection procedure. It merely means that the borderline has to be set at a correspondingly higher level to admit the same proportion as before.

But the only really satisfactory solution must involve a change of attitude, and the elimination of the competitive atmosphere. If there were enough grammar-school provision, or sufficiently attractive alternative schooling, to satisfy parental demands, and if intelligence tests were used—not as a crucial component of a one or two days' examination—but merely as a contribution to a record card which was considered as a whole in making allocations, the incentives to coach and the consequent difficulties would vanish.

VII

The Measurement of Attainment

The Marking of Essay-type Examinations. The measurement of attainment is not a new enterprise. It forms part of the ordinary give-and-take of the classroom. Answers to questions provide some indication of pupils' readiness to pass on to new work, and in written form they allow boys and girls to give considered evidence on their own behalf through responses which their teachers can assess at their leisure. For these reasons, tests of educational attainments are included in the selection procedure.

Over the decades since selection for grammar schools was based almost wholly on the traditional type of examination in English and Arithmetic, quite notable changes have occurred both in the methods of teaching these subjects, and in the techniques of recording and analysing statistics obtained from examination results. These changes are now reflected in modifications in the form and the content of scholastic examinations; and part of the current controversy as to selection procedures is linked with variations in the degree to which the tests reflect older or newer techniques of teaching, of test construction or of test reporting. Discussions of evidence as to the relative merits of new and old have passed through various phases, and tests once described as 'new-type' are now more often called 'objective' or 'standardized', to distinguish them from the older examinations which were subjective in the sense that the questions asked and the answers accepted were determined subjectively by the personal decision of their author, and unstandardized in the sense that evidence was not available as to the relative degree of success or failure in the answers of large samples of pupils of known age or ability. In the words 'objective' and 'standardized' there is thus epitomized much of the history of the testing movement.

The attack on the old type of examining came from two quarters: (i) from those who challenged the subjectivity of its marking and (ii) from those who criticized the narrow range of ability which it sampled.

The first was one of the fruits of the 19th-century movement for the scientific study of education. The second was supported at a slightly later date by the analysis of curriculum content undertaken under the influence of the theories of learning developed by Thorndike and his followers.

Discussion of the inconsistency and element of chance in teachers' marks came in the first place from the developing science of statistics, and for early evidence one must turn to the publications of the Royal Statistical Society. Edgeworth (1888, 1890), for example, writing of results obtained by Bryant and himself, drew attention to the errors attributable both to the idiosyncrasies of examiners and to the limitations of their sensitivity to differing degrees of merit. By the early 1900's Dearborn (cf. Starch, 1916) was writing of variability in the range of marks given by different examiners within the same school system as well as by different instructors to the same class. From this type of evidence came a clear challenge to the supposition that subjectively determined marks (whether on a percentage basis, or in the form of literal categories such as A to E) could be interpreted as anything other than an expression of the marker's personal opinion.

By the 1910's Starch and Elliott had carried the challenge one step further. They arranged that two English papers written by high-school pupils should be photostatically reproduced and marked by 142 teachers of English. The marks which were given ranged from 64 to 98 for one paper and from 50 to 98 for the other with median marks of 88·2 and 80·2, and probable errors of 4·0 and 4·8. A year later (in 1913) similar results were published for the marking of a high-school paper in Geometry by 118 teachers of Mathematics and for the marking of a comparable History paper by 70 teachers of History, the probable errors in these cases being 7·5 and 7·7 respectively.

Attempts were next made to take account of differences in the relative values placed by different instructors on different aspects of a given paper. After full discussion the mean variation of the grades of ten instructors still remained as large as that of the marks given by teachers in different institutions. An adjustment to meet the fact of differences in the average of the marks given by different examiners to the same series of papers reduced the mean variation of the scores from 5·3 to 4·3. By asking seven instructors each to re-mark a set of his own papers after an interval the mean variation was reduced to 2·2 points, though in several instances the second mark differed by as much as ten or fifteen points from the first mark.

These early studies by Starch and his collaborators set the pattern for many subsequent investigations. The techniques employed by research workers have increased in complexity down the decades; but in essentials their findings remain unchallenged. Their importance merits a brief survey of supporting evidence over the last forty years.

Representative Studies on the Marking of English Essays. Before the end of the third decade extensive studies had been made of marking and re-marking essays with and without the aid of 'scales' consisting of selected samples of children's work to which previously agreed values had been given; and correlation techniques had already been applied to the analysis of results. Hudelson (1923), reported from the scoring of 108 narrative compositions (with the use of the Nassau scale) by eight judges on two occasions at an interval of thirty-seven days and obtained a correlation of 0·825 between the median scores of the eight judges on the two occasions. Forty-two days later the same judges re-marked the same essays (with reference to the Harvard-Newton Narration Scale), and the correlations of the median scores with the previous ones were somewhat lower, averaging 0·70.

These findings were confirmed by a later investigation reported in the same volume in which the experiment was repeated with over 400 pairs of specimens of four different types of essay—narratives, descriptions, expositions, and argumentative compositions—written by pupils aged 13 to 15 (Grades 7 to 9). The correlations between the median scores of eight judges on two markings by different scales ranged from 0·41 to 0·80, and averaged 0·64.

At about the same time Boyd (1924), with the collaboration of the research committee of the Educational Institute of Scotland (the professional association of Scottish teachers), was carrying out an investigation on lines more comparable to those reported by Starch.[1] He secured the marking of 26 essays by 271 experienced teachers. These essays had previously been selected by 40 teachers from several thousand compositions as representative of all grades of attainment. All were on the same subject, 'A Day at the Seaside', and were written by pupils of approximately twelve years of age.

In spite of this narrowing of the field, the Scottish results confirmed those obtained in Wisconsin a dozen years earlier. Nineteen of the 26 essays received every mark, or every mark but one; and the markers showed distinct differences in their use of the seven categories, some employing the lower ranges to excess and some only the upper.

These results were discussed in terms of raw scores, percentages and median marks. More elaborate treatment, leading substantially to the same conclusions, was given to material obtained a few years later. In a series of studies on essay reliability, Thomson and Bailes (1926) included the marking by seven experienced judges of a set of essays from 50 boys of about twelve years of age. Six of the seven judges then marked another set of essays from 43 of the same boys. In their analysis of the results they reported the distributions of the marks and their inter-correlations; the latter ranged from 0·42 to 0·85, thus showing considerable discrepancies between many of the markers. Comparable findings from a set of five student teachers marking 48 essays by ten-year-old girls showed a distribution of marks in the various categories similar to that of the experienced head teachers, but lower correlations with the class teacher and with one another (0·52 to 0·73 and 0·34 to 0·67).

The relevance of such findings to public examinations in England was discussed by Valentine and Emmett as early as 1932. In this they recorded not only a low correlation between the order

[1] Earlier studies in Britain of schoolchildren's essays were carried out by a notable group of L.C.C. Inspectors, including Winch, Kimmins and Ballard.

of merit of pupils in entrance examinations and their success in secondary schools four or five years later, but also varying success on the part of scholarship holders in University Honours Schools. Contributory to this variability of performance at both stages may have been what were described as the 'extraordinary' inconsistencies which had been demonstrated between the marking of one examiner and another.

More wholly concerned with the marking of essays and essay-type examinations was the material obtained under the auspices of a series of international conferences on examinations arranged in 1931, 1935 and 1938 by three American organizations—the Carnegie Corporation, the Carnegie Foundation and the International Institute of Teachers College, Columbia University, New York. An English sub-committee reporting to these conferences produced six volumes of which the most important were those by Hartog and Rhodes: *An Examination of Examinations* (1935), *The Marks of Examiners* (a more technical presentation of the same evidence, 1936) and *The Marking of English Essays* (1941). The first two of these presented a systematic comparison of marks given by numbers of experienced examiners to sets of scripts taken from public examinations at the School Certificate stage (History, Latin, French, Chemistry, English), at the stage of entrance to secondary education (Arithmetic and English), and at the level of University Honours (Mathematics and History).

Detailed analyses in terms of difference between examiners, and differences between the same examiners on different occasions, resulted in the confirmation of earlier findings as to variations in assessment not only in humanistic subjects but in subjects such as School Certificate Chemistry and Mathematical Honours. This was reinforced in the first volume by an abbreviated report of comparable studies in France using inter-correlations between marks of different examiners, and in the second by technical discussions by Burt and by Rhodes as to the applicability to such studies of factorial analysis and analysis of variance.

A subsidiary study of the effect of different marking schemes, together with earlier observations on the same topic by Starch and Boyd, prepared the way for Hartog's next inquiry. In the first experiment (1935 and 1936) a series of 75 essays from a Special

Place Examination, whose original marks had ranged from very poor to very good, was marked by ten examiners in terms of general impression; a second comparable set was marked in terms of details such as quantity, quality and control of ideas (50 marks), vocabulary (15), grammar and punctuation (15), structure of sentences (10), spelling (5) and handwriting (5). The analytic set of marks showed a smaller spread, and smaller differences between the averages awarded by different examiners. However, for individual candidates differences as high as 63% were reported from marking by impression, and 52% when marking by detail. Thus no greater precision of marking was obtained by deliberate attention to details rather than to general impression.

In the second experiment, reported in 1941, Hartog arranged for six essays by 100 candidates of School Certificate age to be marked independently by eight examiners for the categories: spelling, punctuation, grammar, vocabulary, sentence structure and general impression. To these was added a seventh grading for 'sense' which, it was thought, might prove productive of greater stability in marking. Elaborate treatment of the results by reduction to standard scores, with the use of analysis of variance and factorial analysis, reaffirmed earlier evidence as to the lack of agreement among examiners both with one another and with their own standards of five months before. It also did not demonstrate the superiority of marking for sense over the other categories employed.

Two other investigations in the same decade presented quite comparable findings. Cast (1939–40) had 12 examiners each mark 40 essays by 15-year-old central-school girls according to four methods, including general impression, Burt's analytic scheme, Hartog's suggestion of 'the writer's achievement of her aim', and the marker's own preferred scheme. Correlational analysis and analysis of variance showed great variations between markers; for example the minimum average range—that for the analytic method—was about 35% of the total marks. A Scottish inquiry (Morrison and Vernon, 1941) similarly compared the very detailed, and allegedly objective, scheme of marking proposed by Steele and Talman (1936) with ordinary analytic + general impression marking of the same essays written by 11-year pupils.

The average correlation between 5 examiners was somewhat higher for the former (0·805) than for the latter set of marks (0·715); but reliabilities, obtained by re-marking one group of essays, were the same for both marking methods, and discrepancies between the averages and ranges of marks awarded by different examiners were much the same for both.

Several post-war investigations by Wiseman (1949), Finlayson (1951), Nisbet (1955) and Edwards Penfold (1956), dealing with essays written for the selection examination, largely reinforce the following conclusions: (i) that it is impossible to secure a high degree of consistency or reliability in the marking of essays as from one marker to another, or by the same marker from one occasion to another. According to Edwards Penfold, even when the significant differences between the means of several examiners (who would have to be employed in marking all the scripts of a large age-group) are eliminated, very serious variations remain in their opinions of the mark to be awarded to any individual candidate; (ii) that efforts to raise the reliability to a 'respectable' level by the adoption of analytic marking schedules, or by previous consultation between markers, make practically no difference. There is little point in quoting further correlations since, as pointed out by Vernon and Millican (1954), the level depends so largely on the heterogeneity of the examinees in respect of essay writing. For example, the average agreement between markers of 11+ candidates is typically around 0·80, whereas with selected groups of School Certificate candidates or university students it may be 0·50 or even lower.

One study which did yield some improvement was that of McMahon (1953) in Cornwall, who showed that by supplying markers with specimen graded essays to cover the whole range of ability, their inter-correlation could be raised to well over 0·9. However, this method has inherent difficulties for selection purposes. It involves a single composition subject for all children, and a good deal of trial and analysis are necessary to produce new specimens for a new subject in the following year. A more practicable scheme was evolved by Robertson in Devon.

Burt (cf. Hartog and Rhodes, 1936) had already put forward the concept of the 'true' mark as being the pooled judgement of an infinite number of markers. It was recognized in other fields of psychology that the random errors occurring in the estimates of a single judge are largely cancelled out when the judgements of a number of judges are pooled. Robertson proposed that four independent markers should take part, using general impression marking (a quick method, so that four markers could mark as quickly as one by analytic methods), the aggregate mark being adopted as the final score. This was then treated like a test 'raw score', age-allowances being applied and the score converted to a 'quotient'. Markers had to satisfy one criterion: a reasonably high mark re-mark correlation. In other words, they must be self-consistent.

Details of this study were reported by Wiseman (1949). Correlations as high as 0·946 and 0·910 were obtained when the total pooled marks on two occasions at an interval of three months were compared. Similar figures, up to 0·96, were obtained by Finlayson and Nisbet in later experiments along the same lines. Thus by this device the inherent subjectivity of essay-marking can be reduced to reasonable proportions, in examinations where the range of pupil-ability is wide.

Criticism of Narrowness of Sampling. The adequacy of the sampling of ability provided by essay-type examinations was first called into question by inquiries into the degree of stability of the performance of the same candidates from one occasion to another. Very full consideration of this was undertaken as early as 1921 in a study reported by Hudelson (1923), in which over 400 13–18-year-old children wrote essays on 32 different topics, chosen to be representative of various adolescent interests and experiences. Each composition was marked for general merit by the pupils' teachers and by seven other experienced teachers, with continuous reference to samples of levels of performance given in published sets of representative compositions. Even on closely similar pairs of topics, correlations between the median scores awarded by eight judges averaged only 0·77 (range 0·69 to 0·84). Hudelson wished to discover the essay subject which for these pupils produced the most uniformly high performance, and the subjects which evoked the most typical performance. But the main interest of his report lies in its evidence as to the variations of performance by pupils at all stages, both on topics of differing types and on topics of similar appeal. Consistency in performance was not high. No one composition could be regarded as a full sampling of a candidate's ability; and the younger the pupil the more unpredictable seemed to be the nature of the topics that would appeal to him.

In an Edinburgh inquiry reported nearly thirty years later Finlayson (1951) collected evidence of a comparable nature. He offered to pupils of about twelve years of age the choice of one topic out of four on two occasions at a week's interval. Variations in subjects selected were considerable and only 41·5 per cent out of 850 children made the same sort of choice in the two instances. A random sample of two essays by each of 197 of these pupils was then marked by six experienced teachers. Results were available, therefore, for the variability between markers, and their self-consistency on re-marking. But here we are concerned with the pupils' consistency of performance at two essays, and the correlation for a typical marker averaged only 0·691, while for the pooled sets of six marks it was 0·863. This indicates a tendency to greater variations among pupils at different topics than between markers marking the same topic—a finding which was confirmed by Vernon and Millican's (1954) analysis of adult students' essays. Perhaps the most stringent test of consistency is the correlation between different pools of markers marking different essays: Finlayson's figure for two essays marked by two independent sets of 3 markers was 0·786. His very thorough investigation includes an analysis of variance of all these sources of variation and their interactions.

Wiseman (1956) also studied the consistency of different essays marked by different sets of 4 markers, obtaining a coefficient approximating to 0·9. Although this still allows considerable variations in children's results, it is not unlike the figure that is found when pupils take two different objective English tests, say a Moray House and a National Foundation test. We may conclude then that it is feasible to include the essay in selection examinations, but that it is desirable to have a minimum of 3 essays from each pupil, each marked by 3 markers, if a reliability closely comparable to that of objective tests is to be achieved. It should go without saying that, when several different batches of markers are needed to cope with the numbers of scripts, their means and distributions should be made equivalent. Admittedly a scheme along these lines would be difficult to organize in areas where the age-group is large, but a great saving can be effected by marking only the scripts of a border-zone group—say those with average quotients from 10 points above to 10 points below the borderline.

The Exclusion of Essays, and their Validity in Selection. During the 1930's the essay was largely abandoned in selection examinations. By 1946 only 37 out of 106 Authorities were using it (N.U.T., 1949), and these were, on the whole, the more conservative ones, since only 1 of the 37 used objective tests in addition. This arose, partly as a reaction to the evidence we have summarized on the unreliability of marking, and partly because of the greater convenience of administering objective tests. In addition there were widespread doubts as to the educational value of trying to train average and duller pupils in this highly complex skill. It was open to such abuses as teaching children whole essays, or sets of flowery phrases, by heart for reproduction in the examination.

On the other hand there were soon forthcoming serious criticisms of the exclusion of the essay, particularly from grammar-school teachers. It was argued that, in selecting children for a grammar-school course, we must be satisfied of their competence in the two basic skills in English, reading comprehension and the ability to write connected sentences. The objective test may measure the first, but it does not measure the second. The notion of measuring ability in English by a test in which the child may be required only to underline words is particularly repugnant to many teachers.

Further criticisms were directed against the backwash effect of testing English purely by multiple-choice test exercises, whose seriousness we have already admitted in Chapter IV. It can be argued that going back to the essay would produce equally undesirable, even if different, effects on junior-school teaching. But this is less likely to occur if the essay is added to the objective test, not substituted for it. Clearly we should not attempt to enforce composition writing in the case of below average children; but it should be possible for the junior schools to give them some training in the writing of simple sentences, while encouraging the abler children to undertake more elaborate and creative writing, whose relevance to a grammar-school type of education is obvious.

In view of these criticisms, it has been suggested that too much weight may have been attached to the essay's defective reliability. The question of whether a coefficient of 0·7 or ·8 or ·9 is high enough cannot be answered in the abstract. What we really need to know is whether the reliability is so low that adding one or more essays to an otherwise objective battery of tests would lower the overall predictive validity of the tests because of the additional error introduced. McMahon (1953) reports correlations of 0·51, 0·66 and 0·82 between primary-school heads' gradings of their own children's essays and overall success in the grammar school two years later. And several experiments have shown that adding an essay to the ordinary test battery raises the predictive value slightly.

Nisbet (1955) found that an English composition, marked either by an impressionistic method (4 markers) or an analytic method (1 marker) resulted in a small, statistically non-significant, increase in the multiple correlation with secondary-school achievement (0·86 to 0·87). The validity of the essay was comparable to that of some of the objective tests, as may be seen in the following Table, but it appeared to be largely duplicating what was already being measured by the Moray House English test.

	Correlations with overall success after 3 years	
	41 senior secondary pupils	*128 junior sec. pupils*
English composition marked by impression method	0·35	0·59
English composition marked by analytic method	0·47	0·60
Moray House English Test 19	0·52	0·71
Moray House Intelligence Test	0·48	0·56

Note: these coefficients are *not* corrected for homogeneity.

Wiseman (1956), using overall School Certificate results as a criterion, found no fall in validity when essay marks were added to the results of objective tests. For English Literature, however, a significant increase in validity was shown when the essay was added to the battery. A similar significant increase was found for modern-school pupils when the criterion was the school's estimate of ability in written English. The following correlations were obtained in a population drawn from several grammar schools:

Essay	*Obj. Eng.*	*Obj. Arith.*	*Verbal Intel.*	*Total S.C.*	*S.C. Eng. Lang.*	*S.C. Eng. Lit.*
Essay	·614	·609	·652	·431	·286	·364
Obj. Eng.		·631	·751	·334	·486	·359
Obj. Arith.			·744	·425	·142	·134
V. Intel.				·416	·412	·429

He calculated regression coefficients from these correlations and showed that the addition of the essay marks to those of objective English, Arithmetic and intelligence raised the maximum correlation significantly in five cases out of six between this team of tests and various criteria. The criteria included total School Certificate marks, School Certificate marks in English Language, School Certificate marks in English Literature and the school estimate of written English. Two of these increases were statistically significant. Moreover, if the objective English test was dropped instead of the essay, the maximum correlation between the tests and the School Certificate total mark was reduced by a mere ·005 from 0·488 to 0·483 as against a fall from 0·488 to 0·432, namely, ·056, when the essay was dropped.

A further comprehensive study, again using the English mark as a criterion, has been carried out by the West Riding on the pupils of 11 mixed grammar schools (Peel and Armstrong, 1956). As a part of their qualification for entry to these schools, the pupils took an English essay as well as a Moray House objective test of English.[1] After three years in their grammar schools, they were

[1] This was a single essay only, marked by different single examiners in different parts of the county, according to a marking scheme and distribution fixed by the Chief Examiner. It may be presumed that still more favourable results might have been obtained with more thorough sampling, and marking, of essay-writing ability.

examined and assessed for attainment in English and foreign languages. The mean correlations for the 11 schools between the predicting tests and the follow-up English marks are suggestive of the value of the essay as an ingredient in the entry examination. The correlations are not corrected for selection.

	Mean correlation with English mark 3 years later
English Composition	·43
Moray House English Test	·47
I.Q.	·40

The full data are published elsewhere, and extracts are given in Appendix A; but here are the correlations for one school which is fairly representative of the general picture obtained from all eleven schools:

		2	3	4	5
1	English Composition	·47	·27	·44	·38
2	M.H. English Test		·43	·56	·31
3	I.Q.			·43	·38
4	English follow-up				·66
5	Modern Languages follow-up				

Inspection of these tables suggest that the Moray House objective English test is a slightly better overall predictor of English than the essay. But these two measures of English cannot be compared without taking account of the inter-correlations between the three entry tests of 0·47, 0·27 and 0·43. It will be noted that the English essay overlaps the intelligence test to a lesser extent than does the objective test of English; hence when an intelligence test is used, the essay is likely to add more to its predictions than can the objective English. This is brought out by the following table of maximum correlations for the combination of all 3 predictors, and for each pair of predictors in turn:

	r_m
Intelligence + Essay + M.H. English	0·59
Intelligence + Essay	0·56
Intelligence + M.H. English	0·55
M.H. English + Essay	0·54

Obviously there is little to choose, and the results vary somewhat from school to school. Nevertheless in 7 out of the 11 schools studies, the results follow this same pattern.

In conclusion it should be admitted that there still exists some disagreement among psychologists who favour, or oppose, the re-introduction of the essay into selection examinations. The former argue: (i) that it is likely to produce some increase in validity, particularly in areas where intensive test-coaching is practised; (ii) that its inclusion will reduce the harmful backwash effects of purely objective English testing, and (iii) that it would satisfy a large number of teachers and promote teacher-co-operation and parent-understanding. The latter urge: (i) that any improvement is so small as to be hardly worth the additional administrative complexities and expense, and (ii) that there are risks of serious unreliability and inconsistency except under very carefully controlled conditions. Finally (iii) they believe that children's skill in written expression can be developed by means less formal than the set composition, and that the modern types of objective English test can sample such skills adequately (cf. Edwards Penfold, 1956; Fleming, 1947–50). To this topic we now turn.

The Development of Objective Tests of English and Arithmetic. The natural outcome of the many investigations of the unreliability of marking and the narrowness of sampling of essay-type examinations which we have summarized was a search for more adequate methods of assessment. The growth of 'new-type' tests is related on the one hand to changes in the interpretation of what is involved in the mastery of a subject, and on the other hand to developments in the technique of mental measurement. The history of the former belongs to the field of research into the content and the procedures of teaching. It engaged the activities of psychologists like Courtis, Starch, Thorndike and Burt in the first decades of the 20th century. From their surveys of the abilities of schoolchildren there came an admission of the range of individual differences; and this was followed by inquiries into the origins of these differences and by attempts to understand their relationship to adult social requirements in counting, reading, spelling, word usage, etc. From such studies there came also a large body of information as to the nature of the activities formerly thought of in quite general terms as reading, counting and composition. It was realized that the mastery of each could be described in terms of a considerable number of clearly defined steps, stages or skills, and a beginning was made in the devising of instructional materials to ensure that every pupil had the chance of learning each type of skill. At the same time, attempts to understand the nature of the mistakes made by unsuccessful pupils led to a revival of interest in proposals for the individualizing of instruction. Changes in classroom methods were supported by an emphasis on the need for activity in learning; and writers of text-books, following the best current practice, began to make provision for silent reading, for the completion of assignments, and for self-instructive and self-corrective procedures in a variety of subjects (cf. Fleming, 1952).

The challenge to the teaching methods of the 1910's had been based on the findings of the early standard tests devised by psychologists for the first surveys of attainment. By the 1930's the schools were leading the way and the more analytic procedures then accepted by teachers were reflected in tests of a new kind. In the 1950's the contents of modern tests still owe much to the schools and reflect the methods followed by expert teachers in the fields both of Arithmetic and English.

The development of skill in written expression is, for example, now fostered by highly diversified methods based on some knowledge of the nature of the difficulties experienced by pupils at differing levels of attainment in the different sections of the subject. The growth of ability in quantitative thinking is now facilitated by a carefully graduated series of mathematical experiences, likewise based on fuller knowledge of the children's own approach and of the nature of the work, and designed to permit the gradual development both of understanding and of skill.

Modern testing in both subjects requires for its content a sampling of these diversified skills. It has therefore come to be clearly defined and analytic rather than indeterminate in character.

It was further recognized that each item in a test should make its own separate contribution to the total assessment. To this may be attributed the substitution of many short questions for the longer exercises which had included a variety of unanalysed activities at differing levels of difficulty.

The differences between old-type tests and new-type tests do not, however, lie merely in the length of the answers they require. They are found rather in the form in which the questions are put; and changes in this are a direct consequence of the search for a type of examination which can be marked by a number of examiners without disagreement as to its quality or the degree of correctness of individual items.

Many differences in opinion between examiners in English or Arithmetic had been caused by differences of emphasis on the constituent elements included in long indeterminate exercises. A large number of short questions was the solution offered in the 1910's and the early 1920's.

Add:

342	543	649	243	304	875
457	212	321	212	291	963
515	362	201	714	300	812
—	—	—	—	—	—

What was the name of the boy?
Why did the boy run away?
Where did he go? etc. etc.

Fuller analysis of content was, however, followed by awareness of differences still remaining, in difficulties within sets of sums which looked alike, and in length and character of response to questions which appeared similar. The next step was taken not only through more careful gradation of questions in Arithmetic, English spelling and vocabulary, but also through the rearrangement of questions in either subject in such a way that they invited from all pupils replies of a similar length, with the elimination as far as possible of differences in skills extraneous to achievement such as rate of writing in a test of word-knowledge, word-usage, reading-comprehension, or problem-solving.

This new style of objective testing took various forms:

I. *Limited but otherwise uncontrolled responses in writing.*

Simple recall questions.

Answer the following questions in one word.

Completion.

Certain words in the story have been missed out. Write them in.

II. *Controlled responses.*

Completion.

Certain words in the story (or the sentence) have been missed out. Alongside are four (or five) possible words. Look for the one which fits in best, and draw a line under it.

Multiple Choice.

Alongside each question are four (or five) words, sets of words, numbers, diagrams or pictures. Find the one which best answers the question and draw a line under it, etc.

Assistance in the constructing and the perfecting of these items owed much to contemporary developments in the field of intelligence testing, in particular to acceptance of the principle of age-performance popularized by Binet in the first two decades, and to discussions of test reliability and validity which followed the use of group tests in the 1920's and the 1930's. The concept of age-performance implied that the suitability of an item can best be determined by trying it out on children comparable to those for whose testing it has been devised. An item is a valid sample of a certain skill in Arithmetic if pupils succeeding in that item also succeed in that skill in general, and if failures in either are failures in both. A test as a whole is a valid measure if its total results accord highly with those obtained from tests believed to be already valid measures in that field.

These techniques are now applied to all tests which can lay claim to the title objective. Only through their use can testers avoid the ambiguity in phrasing which invites disagreement as between pupils of equal competence or irrelevant methods of answering. Only through these procedures can the correctness or incorrectness of any answer be determined independently of the subjective opinion of an examiner; and only through such prior testing can items be arranged in an approximate order of difficulty related to the actual performance of pupils. (The word 'approximate' is used advisedly. Each pupil brings to each item a unique experience and an attitude all his own, and these, as well as the content of the item, are among the determiners of success.) It is important too that procedures in administration should be clearly formulated.

Tests such as these are typical of the late 1920's and the 1930's. They have resulted in series such as those from Moray House in which there is not only a more expert and extensive sampling of pupils' performance than that available from essay-writing or long exercises, but consistency of response is established from one occasion to another of the order represented by correlation coefficients of 0·95, and consistency of marking as between one marker and another and one occasion and another to a degree indicated by correlation coefficients of 0·99 or 1·0.

Important changes have also occurred during this century in the methods of expressing or reporting on the results of tests of attainment. It was early recognized that teachers and examiners vary so widely in the averages and ranges of marks they award that neither letter grades, percentages or other numerical assessments, nor verbal descriptions (excellent, fair, backward, etc.) carry any meaning beyond the confines of the classroom in which they are awarded, and permit no comparison as between one class or one school and another. The standardized tests of attainment published in Britain between the wars (e.g. Ballard's, Burt's, Schonell's) followed the same principles of reference to age levels as did the Binet scales. And though these Educational Ages and Educational Quotients were of considerable help to the educational psychologist and to the teacher in interpreting test results, they were misleading for much the same reasons as are M.A.s and I.Q.s (cf. Chapter VI). Hence the results of attainments tests used nowadays in selection, such as the Moray House and National

Foundation, are expressed as standard scores (which are loosely referred to as English and Arithmetic Quotients). That is, each pupil's score is converted, by the table of norms, to a scale with a mean of 100 for all children born in the same month as himself, and a standard deviation of 15.

Since the second world war, still further developments have taken place in the form and content of some objective tests[1]—changes which go a long way to meet the criticisms that new-type items are unduly analytic, or that they encourage excessive coaching in mere ticking and underlining. This type of response is still useful in sections of a test involving the interpretation of consecutive passages of prose or poetry (silent reading), in tests of arithmetical vocabulary, or of English word-meaning, word usage and the like. In all such instances, other activities such as handwriting or the construction of sentences have been judged to be unnecessary skills whose inclusion would detract from the measurement desired. But in other sections, such as the testing of ability to present ideas in correct literary form or to perform certain definite operations in Arithmetic, the multiple-choice form is abandoned; yet objectivity is still secured by limiting the content of each item. The following are some examples.

I. *Limitation of content, with opportunities for accuracy or inaccuracy in form.*

Below is another part of the story; but in this part the order of the sentences has been mixed. Read the sentences and arrange them in your mind in the right order. Then copy them carefully and fully in that order below. The first one is begun for you.

Have you a good memory? In each of the sentences below parts of some of the words have been missed out. Think what each word should be and write it in full on the dotted line to the right.

Write a sentence giving a good reason for believing that Australia was the country to which Tom was going.

The next two sentences are taken from a letter Tom wrote

[1] For example the Cotswold Series (Fleming, 1955), and many of the recent National Foundation tests.

home to his mother. They have some mistakes in them. Read them carefully. Think what the mistakes are and write the two sentences correctly below.

On this page you are to multiply or divide. Finish each line by writing the answer which you believe to be correct. Be sure to write each answer in full.

II. *Limitation of form with an invitation to variety in interpretation.*

What do you think Tom said when he reached the top of the hill? Write one sentence giving the exact words which you think he would use and also telling how he said them.

Look at this chart. Which school scored 40% of the score made by East Pont?

How many fewer girls than boys in that school were under 5 feet in height?

All such exercises are objective in the sense that they imply prior analysis of content or subject-matter, that the correctness of their answers has been determined by experiments with pupils of comparable age and experience, and that the nature of the wording is such that only a reply of a definite sort is acceptable. Thus although there is some subjectivity in their marking, it has been reduced to a point at which the degree of agreement between competent examiners is represented by correlations of 0·98 to 0·99, and retest reliabilities reach 0·95.

As yet we look for conclusive evidence from comparative experiments to show whether they are superior in validity to the more mechanical and rigid objective tests of the 1930's. But such researches as those of Mitra (1954), and the National Foundation (Pidgeon and Yates, 1957) have given promising results.

The Use of Unstandardized Examinations. Despite the efforts of psychologists, just mentioned, to develop flexible yet accurate tests of attainments, all such tests are still widely criticized by educationists for their backwash effects. Some Authorities have continued to employ old-type examinations throughout the past thirty or more years. Many of these examinations are likely to have been highly unreliable and inaccurate. Yet recent experiments have indicated that, under certain conditions, their predictive validity can be as high as, or even slightly higher than, that of Moray House objective attainments tests.

In the best known, and most fully documented investigation —that of McClelland (1942)—the 'qualifying examination' gave the highest single correlation with later secondary-school success (cf. Appendix A). This examination consisted of an essay, answers to questions on a passage which was read silently, parsing and analysis, dictation and spelling, along with the rewriting of an incorrect passage. To these were added exercises reminiscent of early standard tests: the combining of three short sentences into one, the giving of definitions, of opposites, and of nouns corresponding to verbs. In Arithmetic the test included only a set of ten questions to be answered mentally, and seven written problems. It should be noted that the whole of these examinations were marked by one experienced examiner, hence any unreliability due to variations of standards between markers was eliminated.

In recent inquiries in the West Riding described by Emmett (1954), the county examination in English and Arithmetic showed up slightly better than objective tests in the same subjects. In the grammar schools the unstandardized examinations correlated 0·74 and 0·77 with success, whilst objective tests correlated 0·72 and 0·74 respectively with the same criterion. The intelligence test, however, again proved itself the best single predictor. Similar follow-up results were obtained in the secondary modern schools, where success was better predicted than in the grammar schools, even after the correlations had been corrected for the wider range of ability. Again Richardson (1956) obtained correlations of 0·74 and 0·79 between 'home-made' English and Arithmetic examinations and achievement in Plymouth grammar schools after 1 and 2 years, that is coefficients at least as high as those normally found for Moray House tests (cf. Appendix A).

Dempster (1954) points out that, in the conventional standardized arithmetic test, the first—mechanical—section is almost purely a test of speed of work, and suggests that the second—problem—section should include more difficult questions with a longer time limit. This is borne out by Sutherland's (1952) follow-up study in which there was little to choose between the predictive value of different types of Arithmetic test, but slightly superior correlations were obtained by an untimed test consisting of fairly long problems.

However, it certainly does not follow that all old-type examinations would be equally effective. Indeed it is likely that those which do work well have benefited considerably from the experience gained in half a century's investigation of the improvement of teaching procedures and of techniques of test construction.[1] In Emmett's investigation, much care was given to their construction. There were two English papers lasting 65 minutes altogether, and two Arithmetic papers lasting 55 minutes. 'The first English paper was of a general nature, the second was an essay. The Arithmetic papers contained questions in mechanical and problem arithmetic, appreciably more difficult than those in the standardized Arithmetic tests. Age allowances of approximately 1% of the maximum possible mark per month were applied to the marks.'[2]

The fact that old-type unstandardized examinations in English and Arithmetic, when combined with standardized intelligence tests, lead to much the same efficiency as does a battery consisting wholly of objective tests suggests that more use may be made of well-constructed examinations, particularly in order to ring the changes and so prevent the teaching of these subjects in the

[1] It is noteworthy that the old-type tests which have been followed up have usually been longer than the new-type, and that the criteria with which they have been compared (school marks and examinations) were no doubt more similar in form to old-type than to new-type selection tests. Thus they start with a slight advantage on two counts.

[2] In a personal communication, Mr Armstrong of the West Riding elaborated the procedure further. The English and Arithmetic examinations were in the hands of two Chief Examiners. 'Each drew up his own paper and marking scheme, and tried it out in an area, and after analysis sent the final draft to the Central Examinations Council for approval. Each then selected a representative area, marked the scripts, modified the marking scheme if necessary, and provided a distribution to which the 10 Assistant Examiners allotted to each paper were expected to approximate. If there was a big discrepancy in an Assistant Examiner's marking, his scripts were re-marked by one of the two Chiefs.' A separate follow-up of the essay section of the English examination has been described earlier in this Chapter.

primary school from becoming too stereotyped. At the same time, many psychologists would hold that the risks of going back to outmoded and thoroughly unreliable techniques cannot be ignored, and that it is likely that the modern new-type test will in the long run prove to be a more satisfactory instrument.

VIII

The Use of Primary School Marks and Teachers' Estimates

THERE ARE numerous excellent reasons for making use of primary-school marks or teachers' judgements of their pupils instead of, or at least as a supplement to, external tests or examinations:

1. Such judgements can be based on the pupils' performance over a year, or several years, instead of on what they do at an examination lasting at most two days, and often consisting of three 45-minute tests only.

2. They reflect the children's normal work under everyday conditions, whereas the examination is often done under considerable emotional strain. Not only are some children adversely affected, but others who have received skilful coaching at home or out of school may do better than they deserve.

3. We have seen that any form of external examination is liable to have bad effects on the curriculum and teaching. If internal assessments could be substituted, each school could teach its pupils in the manner which appeared most desirable from the educational and psychological standpoints.

4. A good teacher should have a fuller knowledge of children's persistence, intellectual promise and other qualities relevant to successful secondary-school work than can be given by a limited battery of objective tests, or other purely written examinations.

We therefore find an increasing number of Local Authorities considering a child's previous school record or head teacher's report in their efforts to determine the type of secondary education for which he is best suited. Of 106 Authorities who forwarded information to the Consultative Committee of the N.U.T. in

1949, 94 used reports or records in some way, either for all pupils, or for those falling in the border-zone, or for special cases with irregular results. Few Authorities felt sufficient confidence in school assessments to justify attaching as much importance to them as to marks obtained in external examinations. But since that time, some have arranged to give them equal weight with attainments tests, and a few have actually discarded the attainments tests in their favour.

A number of different types of information provided by the primary schools may be distinguished:

(*a*) Order of merit rankings, or marks, for particular school subjects, given either separately or combined.

(*b*) Orders of merit or other ratings on 'general suitability', or on other qualities relevant to secondary-school success.

(*c*) Gradings on point or letter scales for ability at different subjects, for special abilities and interests, and for personal qualities such as perseverance, initiative, reliability and self-confidence. These are usually collected on some form of cumulative record card.

(*d*) A more general or qualitative report by the head teacher on each candidate's strengths and weaknesses.

Neither (*c*) nor (*d*) can readily be quantified in such a manner as to be comparable for all candidates from all schools. Thus they are used chiefly by panels, or by grammar-school heads, for gaining an overall picture of individual children. We will consider such procedures in Chapter IX, and confine the present discussion to (*a*) and (*b*).

Difficulties in Using School Marks and Estimates. Having outlined the advantages, it is desirable straight away to list the common defects or disadvantages, and then to note how far these can be overcome.

1. Not only the teacher's general impression of a child's suitability, but also the marks he or she gives to his school work, may be prejudiced by his personal reactions to the child. There is ample psychological evidence of the inability of any human judge to keep separate his assessments of intellectual traits from those of moral or social traits. That is, he may unwittingly be

influenced by the child's cheekiness, bullying or delinquent tendencies, dirtiness, troublesomeness in class, and their opposites. This is particularly dangerous in very small schools, where a single teacher may have been responsible for almost the whole of the child's instruction. But even in large schools where numerous teachers have contributed to the record card, or have been consulted by the head in drawing up his assessment, the combined judgement may be fallible. In other words, some schools are likely to provide very much better judgements than others, and unfortunately there is no sure technique of determining the inaccurate ones and excluding them. This means then that judgements in general cannot be perfectly reliable and valid, though it does not necessarily imply that they are inferior in these respects to other methods of assessment.

2. As soon as parents get to know of the importance attached to teachers' judgements or marks, the teachers become liable to so much pressure that they often prefer not to accept this responsibility. The Chief Education Officer for Bournemouth recently pointed out that, if selection was based largely on teachers' estimates, there was a danger that present-day complaints about tests would be replaced by still more violent complaints about favouritism and victimization by teachers. This difficulty too is more serious in small schools, e.g. in rural areas, where the one or two teachers concerned are known personally to all the parents. In King's inquiry (described in Chapter IV), several teachers thought that the use of assessments would complicate their relations with parents and with pupils. More than half did not believe that the accuracy of prediction could be improved by them, and only a very small minority was willing to abolish external tests altogether.[1] Despite the harmful effects of tests on teaching, they clearly help to protect the teacher. However, in certain areas where tests and estimates have been regularly used for some years, no special difficulties with parents have arisen.

3. It is impossible for teachers to make adequate allowances for age differences, and we have seen that this greatly handicaps the

[1] The same point is made in an article, 'Selection in Practice', by a junior-school teacher in *The Times Educ. Suppl.*, July 20th, 1956, p. 958.

younger candidates in an age-group. Even if they are warned of it, or advised to add so many marks, say for each month below 11:6, they will tend to vary widely in their adjustments. Indeed it is better for them not to try, since appropriate allowances can readily be added later in the Education Office.

4. Though evidence is lacking, it also seems likely that teachers' judgements will be more affected by social class than are objective tests, particularly intelligence tests. The middle-class child will tend to impress the average teacher as being better suited to grammar-school education because of his advantages in vocabulary, his more rapid early progress in reading and number, his more acceptable manners, and the greater likelihood of encouragement by the home. Such reasons may be valid ones (cf. Chapter III); thus the grammar schools may well approve the teachers' recommendations despite their bias. On the other hand some teachers who hold strongly socialist views, or who perhaps themselves come from poorer backgrounds, may over-compensate against middle-class qualities. Thus any Authority which does decide to give greater weight to teachers' judgements should do so with its eyes open.

5. Many school record-cards require the inclusion of objective test scores. Even without this, it is often found in practice that teachers prefer to apply tests, with or without official permission, to guide their judgements. This would seem to vitiate the intention to take primary-school work into consideration as an independent source, or as a substitute for tests. However, we see little harm in this, since most teachers would use the test results mainly for pitching their standards, and would generally put more trust in their own observations of each individual pupil's work than in his test scores. Moreover when tests are given in this manner, there is nothing like the same temptation to 'teach to' them as when they are applied in an external examination.

6. The most serious difficulty is that, however accurate the teacher's assessments of the *relative* merits of his own pupils, he is apt to be highly inaccurate in his standards of *absolute* judgement. He seldom has much opportunity for comparing his pupils with those in other schools, and hence may be far too lenient or far too severe all round. Primary schools themselves,

of course, do vary considerably in the average level and the range of their pupils' abilities, both from one district and from one year to another.[1] But one can hardly expect the head teacher to know just how much better or poorer his school is than the general run. And over and above such natural variations, teachers' judgements of the standards needed for a grammar-school course vary widely. McClelland (1942) quotes figures for teachers' English and Arithmetic marks in twelve schools, which were compared with the same pupils' marks on a uniform pair of objective tests. The average school overmarked its average pupil by 20% (on a scale with a S.D. of about 20). But some schools awarded an average only 2% too high, whereas others ranged up to 35% too high. This is the main explanation for the finding in several older researches (e.g. Valentine & Emmett, 1932; Sutcliffe & Canham, 1944) that the 'raw' marks or judgements provided by a miscellaneous group of primary schools give far lower correlations with subsequent secondary-school success than do marks on external examinations or tests.

However desirable it might seem educationally, therefore, it would be quite impossible to allocate grammar-school places fairly on the recommendation of the primary schools alone. It is essential to have some means of 'calibrating', 'scaling', or 'standardizing' the school estimates, i.e. bringing them to a comparable level.

Validity of Scaled Estimates. When this is done, the evidence for validity is extremely favourable. In McClelland's (1942) investigation, the scaled teachers' estimates gave correlations of the same order as those of the external examinations, and higher than those of the objective attainments tests (cf. Appendix A). The best combination of all the predictors consisted of I.Q. + marks in English and Arithmetic examinations, + teachers' estimates of ability in these subjects. The West Riding have also looked into the validity of such estimates as part of their large-scale inquiry into different parts of the selection procedure. The average of the correlations obtained in 12 grammar schools between overall

[1] Hence it would be grossly unfair to select, say, the best 20% from each separate primary school.

success and various measures of English and Arithmetic were as follows:

	Teachers' Estimates		*School Tests*		*County Exams.*	
	Engl.	*Arith.*	*Engl.*	*Arith.*	*Engl.*	*Arith.*
Average r	·43	·47	·33	·39	·35	·38

These coefficients are, of course, uncorrected for range of ability. The National Foundation for Educational Research has likewise found that as good, if not better, predictions of pupils' success in secondary schools can be obtained from primary head teachers' estimates, when suitably scaled, as from an examination consisting of standardized tests of intelligence and attainments. Richardson (1956) provides further evidence.

In some follow-up studies the validities of primary-school marks or estimates is spuriously high, either because the estimates themselves were not actually employed in making the selection, or because no age adjustments had been applied. However, these pitfalls were avoided in a review of the progress of 550 children attending Northumberland county grammar schools, where the following coefficients (corrected for selectivity) were obtained (Bosomworth, 1953). The most appropriate weightings of the various measures for maximum accuracy of prediction are also shown:

	Scaled Estimates	*Verbal I.Q.*	*Non-Verbal I.Q.*	*E.Q.*	*A.Q.*	*Multiple r*
Validity Coefficient	·855	·852	·676	·869	·830	·918
Beta Weight	·282	·138	·110	·261	·047	

Techniques of Scaling. A number of different schemes have been tried by Local Authorities. The three main types are: A. The Quota Scheme; B. Scaling against Scores on an Objective Test or Battery; C. The West Riding Scheme.

A. The Quota Scheme. This method for allocating children to secondary schools is based upon proposals by Professor C. W. Valentine (1938), and it was recommended by the N.U.T. Committee (1949). To every primary school in a certain area is given an allocation of grammar-school places, based on the performance of the school's pupils at one, or preferably two, intelligence tests. For example, if it is decided that the average intelligence quotient of 116 is the minimum standard in the area for grammar-school admission, and primary school A has 5 pupils with average I.Q.s of 116 and above, then the quota for that school is 5. However, the five children ultimately recommended for transfer to grammar schools are not necessarily the ones with the highest I.Q.s, but those five who occupy the highest places in that school on the basis of their combined scores in the intelligence tests, teachers' assessments, and primary-school marks. The assessments and marks within each school are first converted to standard scores (with an age allowance), and equal weight is then usually given to each component. Note, however, that the estimates and marks need not be limited to English and Arithmetic; they can cover a much wider field of primary-school work.

In spite of the apparent administrative convenience and fairness of the method, it has not been adopted in its entirety by many Authorities. Walsall (cf. Moore, 1948) was the pioneer in its use, and it has there received wide approval from teachers and parents. A similar scheme operates in Derbyshire. One of its difficulties is that schools which submit their children to efficient coaching on intelligence tests can obviously gain a higher quota than schools of the same ability level where coaching has been discouraged. Perhaps this is not so serious in that schools in any one area can usually arrange to follow a common policy, and much of the unevenness can be ironed out if practice tests are given to all schools concerned.

Another objection sometimes voiced is that it is the negation of allocation according to ability and aptitude; it is merely a device for filling the existing grammar-school places with the best of the available children. However, this criticism really applies to all selection procedures, and, as shown in Chapter I, it follows from the fact that in most areas the supply of grammar-school places falls far below parental demands.

Much more serious is the unreliability of the quotas which the system assigns to small schools. Indeed it is clearly inapplicable in areas containing many schools which submit only half a dozen or fewer candidates, since there would be such a large chance element in their capacity to win 0, 1, 2 or more I.Q.s above the borderline. This problem is examined in Appendix C, where it is shown that the quota yielded by one test, or even by a battery of tests, may be very wide of the mark. For example, if one test given to a school with 40 candidates yields a quota of 8 (20%), a second similar test may quite well reduce the figure to 6 or raise it to 10 places. Alternatively, if it could by some means be established that the true or correct quota for that school was 8, the figure indicated even by a couple of intelligence tests might range anywhere from about 5 to 12, though such extreme cases would be the exception; for a typical school the discrepancy would be only 1 or 2 places. If then we consider schools with only 10 candidates, the percentage error is doubled, showing that the obtained quota for small schools is almost meaningless. The inaccuracy would be appreciably reduced by employing attainments as well as intelligence tests for fixing the quota. But then, of course, we should be back more or less where we started, since the schools would naturally cram their pupils to do as well as possible on the attainments tests. The poor reliability of the quota system arises because a percentage is, inevitably, an unreliable statistic, possessing a large Standard Error. Let us turn, then, to other techniques of scaling which are somewhat more accurate because they are based on more reliable data.

B. Scaling against Scores on Objective Tests. Numerous methods have been tried, and the technical details of some of these are discussed in Appendices C and D. However, they may all be regarded as variants of the standard techniques of scaling, which are set out in such text-books as McIntosh (1949) or Vernon (1956). That is to say, the teachers' marks, estimates or rank orders in any one school are compared with the same pupils' scores on an objective test (or set of tests) which has been applied to all the schools in the area; the former are then converted on to the same scale as the latter, either via a percentile graph, or by adjusting their mean and standard deviation. Thus the estimates from a particularly good school, or one which has undermarked its pupils, are shifted up; and those from a poorer or unduly optimistic school are scaled down. Note that the estimates do not normally make any allowance for age; hence they should preferably be scaled against test *scores*, not quotients. Once scaled, they can themselves be turned into quotients or other scores with an age allowance.

The problem of reliability is still a serious one. Any technique is liable to yield scaled estimates which are somewhat too high, or too low, for all the pupils in one school. Indeed in the case of very small schools, accurate scaling is virtually impossible; and it would seem essential to continue to assess their pupils mainly by means of an external battery of attainments tests or examinations, applied either by the Authority or by the grammar school which they feed.[1] But there is no doubt that scaled estimates are more trustworthy than either the original quota scheme, or any system which tries to use unscaled judgements. For example, from the discussion in Appendix C, it would appear that a typical head, who relied on internal school marks and his own unaided judgement of standards, might recommend anywhere from 3 to 15 out of 40 pupils as suitable for grammar school, when the true figure should be 8. Under the quota scheme, the limits of inaccuracy would be 4 or 5 to 12 or 13; but if his estimates were properly scaled, the limits would be reduced to 6 to 10.

The crucial factor in improving the accuracy of scaling is the validity of the external test or tests against which the scaling is done. Thus it is better to use a combination of intelligence, English and Arithmetic rather than intelligence alone, not because school estimates of English may correlate better with an English test, but because this battery is more valid than any single test. We would conclude reluctantly, therefore, that it is inadvisable to dispense with external tests of attainments. Once they have been applied for scaling purposes, they can if desired be largely disregarded and selection can be based mainly on the scaled estimates and intelligence test. But the best policy would seem to be to use

[1] Some account can still be taken of these schools' recommendations by the panel procedure described in Chapter IX.

all the available data to yield the most thorough assessment for each child, while paying more attention to the estimates than to the external attainments quotients. For example, in some instances the estimates may indicate that a child has 'flopped' unduly on one or more tests; more rarely the tests may indicate that he is more (or less) promising than his school believes.

At the same time it might be justifiable to abandon attainments tests in areas where there is reason to believe that they are seriously distorting primary-school teaching, and to scale the estimates (from fair-sized and large schools) on intelligence tests alone, at least temporarily. If two intelligence tests are given and adequate precautions taken against differential coaching, the loss in accuracy is not very large. For example, in Richardson's (1956) research, the validity of estimates scaled on intelligence was 0·764, as compared with 0·791 for the same estimates scaled on intelligence, English and Arithmetic.

Another point to remember is that the retention of attainments tests does help to convince the public that reliance on teachers' judgements is not being abused. We have seen already that many, possibly the majority of, teachers prefer tests, partly for this reason and partly because they realize the difficulties of reaching comparable standards. Some Authorities which do attach considerable weight to estimates have concealed the fact from the parents, and even from the teachers, in order to safeguard the latter from undue pressure. In our view it is better to be as frank as possible regarding the procedures employed. But it can always be emphasized that the final decision is made by the Education Committee rather than by the schools.

In some areas, the Authority encourages or enforces the application of standardized attainments and/or intelligence tests at one or more stages between 7+ and 10+, for entry on record cards. Might not these tests take the place of external attainments tests at 11+? We agree that, when teachers come to give their estimates, the previous tests can act as a guide, and help to maintain some sense of perspective between widely different schools. But it would be too chancy to rely on them alone and to dispense with formal scaling. One other promising alternative relies upon subsequent tests (given in the secondary schools) instead of on previous ones; as this is still in the experimental stage, it is described in Appendix D.

It should be noted that scaling does not necessarily have to be based on objective attainment or other tests. Old-type examinations could equally well be employed, provided that they were applied to and marked uniformly for all schools, and that they were equally valid.

A final problem to consider is what form the estimates should take. Letter grades are far too coarse. But if the schools (particularly those with large numbers) find percentage or other marks having a good spread more convenient to award than rank orders, it is just as easy to scale these, and somewhat more fair to the outstanding pupils. It has often been suggested that teachers should assess 'general suitability', and should give full weight to personality factors, home background and likelihood of parental encouragement, since these highly relevant considerations are largely excluded by conventional selection procedure, except in so far as they are reflected in success at attainments tests. Others, however, consider that the dangers of teachers being influenced by inappropriate considerations are greater than the advantages of giving them freedom to interpret 'suitability' in whatever manner they think best; therefore they would prefer to confine the judgements of marks simply to all-round attainment, or to attainment in specific subjects such as English and Arithmetic. There is some (unpublished) evidence from Northumberland that the latter 'subject' estimates are more valid than the former 'general suitability' estimates. The other factors just mentioned should, rather, be entered on the pupils' record cards and considered, in borderline cases, by the panel procedure recommended in Chapter IX. Incidentally, the adoption of 'subject' estimates meets an objection which is sometimes raised, namely that teachers may be very competent in judging suitability for grammar, but not for technical, schools. If they merely assess attainments, their estimates can be given as much weight in technical-school selection as is normally given to scores on attainments tests.

C. The West Riding Scheme, and Other Methods of Consulting Teachers' Judgements. In several areas (e.g. Hertfordshire and

Wiltshire) there is no formal scaling of primary-school estimates, and yet the grammar-school heads and education officers who decide which children to admit rely largely on statements regarding suitability made by the primary heads in their catchment district. They get to know that the children regarded as border-zone by the head of School A have made good progress in the grammar school in recent years, whereas the head of School B has tended to over-estimate his pupils' capabilities. The procedure in Wiltshire around 1951 (cf. James, 1952) involved visits by a panel to each primary school. The school's candidates were discussed and compared with candidates from previous years. Such information was then considered along with the results of external tests or examinations, and of an interview with each candidate.

Though procedures of this type may satisfy the schools concerned, they seem to us too chancy to be recommended, and too dependent on the standards of judgement and persuasiveness of the primary heads, even when external attainment test results are available as a check. In addition they still do nothing to free the primary schools from the burden of preparing their pupils for such tests, and they do not incorporate proper age allowances.

Recently, however, G. F. Peaker (Staff Inspector for Research at the Ministry of Education) has devised a scheme which does cut out the examining of the great majority of children, while also providing an objective means of equating the estimates provided by different schools. It depends upon the fact that, although different schools send very different proportions to the grammar school, the proportion from the same school changes little from year to year. In fact, a survey of a large number of cases over several years showed that, in two years out of three, the number of grammar-school places obtained by a typical school lies within 4 of its own average (i.e. the standard deviation of places gained by a school seldom exceeds 4). Hence by giving each primary school an initial quota of places equal to the average number gained during the preceding five years, a first approximation to the proper number could be made. To take a concrete instance: a school with an average of 10 places would be entitled to send forward to the grammar school the first 8 on its order-of-merit list. The next 4 in order constitute a border-zone group which, along with similar groups from other schools, would be examined by a committee of teachers, whose main function would be to select one-half of the total group. If however all 4 children from any one school were accepted, it would be necessary for it to put forward for consideration the next 4 on its list. Similarly, if all 4 from any one school were rejected, the next 4 above them would be examined to determine their suitability.

No particular system is laid down for the examination of these border-zone cases. The scheme has been tried experimentally in the Thorne area of West Riding, where there was an age-group of some 800 children in 21 primary schools, of whom some 120 were due to be admitted to one grammar school. The actual selection was based on the customary procedure, using Moray House tests. Peaker's method was applied as an additional shadow scheme to see how its results compared. Two panels dealt with 69 border-zone cases in one day, and gave them non-standardized tests of English and Arithmetic plus an interview, reference also being made to primary heads' reports in doubtful cases.

With the acceptance of 34 of these children, the first adjustment of quotas was completed. But, as would be expected, all 4 children from one school were accepted, and all 4 from another were rejected. Hence a second 'round' was necessary, where a similar procedure was used. A third 'round' could have been added; but in this experiment no discrepancy from the original quota was as large as 8 places (i.e. twice the standard deviation).

The results of the procedure were compared not only with those of the Moray House tests, but also with the allocation indicated by an additional battery of N.F.E.R. tests. Ninety-six children were passed and 636 failed by all three methods, but there were 59 children (7·5%) whose results varied. There were nearly as many disagreements between the two sets of objective tests as between either set and the shadow scheme (actually 3·8% as compared with 5·6%). When the results were compared with performance at the end of the first year in the grammar school, the correlations (appropriately corrected) were all very high: Moray House 0·92, National Foundation 0·90, New Scheme 0·88. It has therefore been decided to adopt the new scheme in this area next year. Though there were at first some doubts among the teachers, regarding the degree of responsibility placed on their judgements, they have now given it their support. Certain difficulties should, however, be noted.

(i) There is the problem of the small school, whose quotas over several years have averaged 0, 1 or 2. The Thorne experiment tried to allow for this by including in its border-zone group any children from small schools who had been recommended by their heads. However, this solution might be unfair to schools where the teacher has unduly high standards.

(ii) The organization and carrying out of successive rounds would be extremely elaborate in large age-groups. If, as a safeguard, not only primary heads but also parents could demand inclusion of their children in the border-zone group, an enormous number of panels might be needed. It may well be that the running of current selection procedures has become over-centralized; but the devolution implied by the West Riding scheme might lead to uncontrollable variations in the methods employed by different panels. For this reason a somewhat different scheme is now being tried in an area where there is a complicated criss-cross pattern of transfer (cf. Appendix D).

(iii) Although in the Thorne experiment the age distribution of those accepted by the scheme was only slightly higher than that of those accepted by the objective tests, there are serious dangers in the absence of any easy and accurate technique of making age allowances.

(iv) Marked changes in the quality of candidates at any one school may occur, particularly with big population shifts. Thus a school might deserve 8 or 10 places more than its initial quota; but if one of its first 4 candidates happened to be rejected by the panel, it would only get 3 places. Linked with this difficulty is the possibility that the schools' standards of judgement might drift when they have no regular external examinations as a check. This too may be met by the supplementary scheme. Meanwhile further trials are needed to bring out fully both the feasibility and fairness of this approach.

IX

Other Techniques used in Selection for Technical Education and in Consideration of Border-zone Cases

Spatial and Mechanical Tests. We have pointed out, in Chapter III, that accurate differentiation of technical from academic aptitude is not possible at 11, nor even at 13, years; though at the same time tests may help to reveal those children with a strong bias in either direction. There has been considerable controversy in the past as to the age at which a spatial or practical ability factor (often termed *k*, or *k* : *m*—spatial-mechanical, by psychologists) can be recognized (cf. Vernon, 1950). However, the work of Peel (1948b, 1949), Emmett (1949) and others shows that the contrast between this factor and the linguistic factor does exist even well before 11; the difficulty is rather that the available tests for younger children fail to give as good predictions of later ability in technical subjects as do tests at, say, 13. It was at first thought that performance tests such as Alexander's (1935) were the best measures of the practical factor. But group paper-and-pencil tests based on non-verbal spatial problems have been found to be as adequate, more reliable, and less time-consuming. Some Local Authorities therefore augment the customary battery of tests of verbal intelligence, English and Arithmetic by one of the spatial tests issued by Moray House or the National Foundation. Unfortunately all *k* tests yet designed have shown themselves to be measures of the *g* or general ability factor first and *k* second. Hence not more than about one-third of able pupils can be effectively allocated to grammar and technical schools at the same level purely on the basis of these ability tests (cf. Watts and Slater, 1950).

With recruits in the Services, and adolescent apprentices, tests of mechanical information have been found valuable in supplementing measures of *k*. But with primary-school children of 10 to 11, who have had little mechanical experience, the use of these or other tests of *m*-factor is unlikely to prove very profitable, or acceptable to teachers and parents. It should be noted also that there are no suitable tests for commercial, agricultural, artistic, domestic or other types of biased secondary course.

Other Authorities who select for both technical and grammar schools at 11+ dispense with non-verbal tests and rely on the three standard tests, but then take account of the views of the parents and advice of the primary teachers in allocating the able children; and there is much to be said in favour of this procedure.

Test of Interests. Educational psychologists have also tried to assess children's interests at this stage, as a means to more objective differentiation of suitability. One of the difficulties here is the instability of interests at such an early age. It might, however, be argued that strong practical interests in a boy at 11 years are likely to wane if he is sent to a grammar school, where such interests have often little to feed on, whereas allocation to a technical high school might ensure their permanence. It is worth noting that in Terman's long-term follow-up of highly intelligent children scientific interests at 10 years and earlier were found to persist into adult life for a high proportion of his subjects.

Peel and Lambert (1948b, 1949) have constructed an interest test of the information type which contrasts 'practical' and 'academic' interests. Follow-up shows moderate validity for the difference-score, P–A, as a measure of practical bias. Fitzpatrick and Wiseman have used a questionnaire type of interest test which yields separate practical and academic scores (Wiseman, 1955). They show that by its use, together with a spatial test, some two-thirds of pupils can be differentiated between technical and grammar, although follow-up data are not yet available. Further work along these lines is desirable: results so far show that interest tests are a promising addition to the technical selection battery.

The possibility of obtaining reliable information from teachers about children's interests should not be forgotten. There are many difficulties in the way, however, as indicated in Chapter VIII. In addition to these general problems, the question of estimating practical abilities and aptitudes is particularly difficult in view of the wide variety of craft curricula in primary schools. If a child has had experience of a craft which involves measurement and some degree of accuracy, then the school may well have useful information for technical selection. If, however, the craftwork is more plastic in nature (e.g. modelling) its relevance is less certain. The possibility of getting information about hobbies, spare-time interests and other background data should be considered. An attempt (Wiseman, 1952) to gather information by means of a record form filled in by the teacher dealing with interests, parental attitudes and vocational ambitions, best and worst school subjects, etc., gave promising results in a factor analysis of correlations of tests of attainments, intelligence, interests and spatial ability.

Measures of Personality. A recurrent theme in criticisms of selection is that the intelligence and objective attainments tests give an advantage to the 'slick and superficial' child. This denunciation is sometimes followed by a demand for the inclusion of measures of such personality qualities as persistence, conscientiousness, perseverance and initiative, or the *X*-factor whose importance was demonstrated by Alexander (1935). These qualities are often listed on school record-cards, and it might seem that the primary-school teacher is in a particularly favourable position to make estimates of them. Experience shows, however, that such ratings are of doubtful value, for two main reasons. In the first place, it is common to find a child displaying a good deal of 'persistence' in one particular lesson, or with a particular teacher, and very little in another lesson or with another teacher. Such traits are largely specific to the particular task or situation at this age. Secondly, teachers' ratings are contaminated with 'halo effect'; those children who show good attainments (and behaviour) are generally rated high on personality factors, and vice versa. Indeed McClelland's (1942) investigation showed clearly that teachers' personality ratings do not add anything to the accuracy of predictions based on tests and estimates of attainment, such as those described in Chapter VIII. The results of any attainment tests given at 11+, particularly those of the 'old-type' pattern, must have been affected by personality traits which are relevant to secondary-school success. Hence, even in the simplest selection programme, personality is certainly not excluded.

Though some suggestions regarding possible objective tests for selection at this stage have been made elsewhere (Vernon, 1953), it is doubtful whether any of them are ever likely to be practicable for widespread application. Even the measurement of a single trait, such as persistence, at a satisfactory level of reliability would involve the employment of a number of lengthy tests, probably mainly individual. Thus, if additional consideration is to be given to personality factors, it is probably best tackled as part of the procedure for dealing with border-zone pupils, as shown below.

The Qualitative Consideration of Border-zone Pupils. If a whole age-group is being allocated in the proportion of around 20% to grammar schools and 80% to modern schools, it is often said that *any* method will correctly pick out the top 10% or so and the bottom two-thirds, and that the real difficulty lies with the intermediate or border-zone cases. This is not quite correct. Even with our very best procedures, 1 of these top 10 (with an average test quotient of 119 upwards) is likely to turn out a misfit in the grammar school, and 1 with a quotient of 105 or below would have been more suitably placed in a grammar than a modern school. And had we used a more old-fashioned or poorer procedure with a validity of, say 0·75 instead of 0·90, then there would probably be 3 misfits in each group.

Nevertheless it is true to state, first, that much more doubt arises over the correct allocation of pupils between such limits than beyond them; and, secondly, that there is relatively little to choose between the validities of any of the current, carefully devised, procedures. They would all pick out nearly—though not quite—the same highs and lows. But they would often give quite diverse decisions in the case of children near the borderline; hence the need to pay special attention to this zone. So far as quantitative selection procedures go, it is impossible to claim that the 113's are appreciably better than the 112's. Teachers, and many parents, are aware of this, and very pardonably object to a purely mechanical and impersonal cut-off which says that the 113's are able enough for grammar school and the 112's are not. They demand therefore that any special circumstances or other qualitative factors bearing on the children's suitability should be taken into consideration in order to improve this discrimination and to minimize any unfairness.

Now in the occupational field, strong evidence has been obtained (cf. Vernon, 1953) that qualitative or clinical consideration of the individual case does not necessarily improve predictions based on quantitative measures, and may even introduce worse inaccuracies. That this is true in educational selection also is indicated by McClelland's (1942) inability to reduce his numbers of 'wrong accepts' and 'wrong rejects' by taking into account health records and other data. Nevertheless it seems to us more important to ensure that maximum justice should appear to be done than to take a rigid stand on statistical findings. To pursue the latter course, indeed, is only too likely to decrease public confidence in the accuracy and fairness of the allocation procedure, and to bring discredit on the work of psychologists and statisticians.

According to Dempster's survey of procedures in 1951, all but a very few Authorities were employing special procedures of one kind or another with border-zone cases. Some two-thirds were seeking information from the children themselves by interview, oral examination or other 'observational' techniques; some made more or less extensive use of record cards or other forms of report from the primary schools; and some combined both methods.

Interviews and Oral Examinations. The child, and sometimes his parents, may be interviewed by the grammar-school head, or by a small panel of teachers. The method is doubtless a convenient one for bringing together all the relevant data and seeing the child as a whole person; and it makes possible the collection of further material on his interests and abilities, and his parents' attitudes. But most psychologists would agree with the N.U.T. Committee of 1949 that interviewing is thoroughly undesirable, for several reasons: (i) It puts a considerable strain on many children, so that the behaviour observed may be quite uncharacteristic; (ii) Interviewers are liable to be impressed by the 'wrong' things such as deportment, dress, accent and the like. Since these largely reflect social class and age, they may in fact help in picking pupils who will adjust well to the grammar school, thus spuriously reinforcing the interviewers' confidence in the soundness of their judgements; (iii) A large amount of evidence from war-time research confirmed psychologists' doubts as to the consistency of interviewers and the validity of their judgements of personality (cf. Vernon and Parry, 1949). So far as interests and suitable home background are concerned, the report of the child's teachers who have known him for several years, despite its imperfections, is much more likely to be trustworthy than the impressions gathered in 15 minutes under highly artificial conditions. Equally to be deprecated are attempts to assess brightness or attainments by a few miscellaneous oral questions. In general, whenever conclusions derived from interviewing 11-year-old children are allowed to outweigh the evidence from test scores and scaled teachers' estimates, the accuracy of prediction is likely to be lowered far more often than it is improved.

A rather better case can be made for the interview in connexion with the late transfer of pupils at 13+. In Devon, for example, a considerable number of boards sit concurrently, their standards being equated by a technique suggested by Drew (1946) for selection for apprenticeship courses. Test results at 11+ and 13+ are available to the boards as well as detailed school reports. The interview itself is only controlled in the sense that previous briefing lays down the general aim and method. Follow-up studies have shown that acceptances under this scheme tend to stay at school longer, and to get higher ratings in the *later* years in grammar school, than do those pupils admitted on test results only.

In Northumberland also it has been found that, under carefully controlled conditions, there may be some value in oral examinations designed to be complementary to the written test, and that occasional children show up better under these circumstances than in written work. Experiments have been in progress for some ten years. At first, rather elaborate interviews were arranged, conducted by experienced head teachers, and designed to assess the child's interest in an academic type of work. Follow-up showed that teachers' scaled assessments were much superior to interview judgements, and the interview has gradually been changed to a more objective type of oral examination. Written as well as verbal answers are given by the children, and the responses to carefully prepared questions tabulated and assessed. Such oral tests have been found to possess good reliability and to yield promising correlations with later success.

In other counties all border-zone pupils in the catchment area a particular grammar school come to that school for one day's of further examination. For example in E. Sussex the procedure varies to some extent from one school to another (which has the advantage that each school gets the sort of pupils it wants, though it would be undesirable if the variations became excessive); but it usually includes an additional composition and an old-type arithmetic paper, plus a short interview with the head which is assigned relatively little weight. Sometimes a teacher takes a small class of candidates in a grammar-school lesson, observes their responses and marks a short written test at the end.[1] In a follow-up of a whole age-group of border-zone admits after 2 years, Carr (1957) was able to prove that the overall mark awarded by each of the 8 grammar schools did add appreciably to the validity of predictions derived from the customary objective tests alone, even when age-corrections were applied.

Group Observational Techniques. A somewhat different method of 'observed activity' has been developed in Devonshire by Wiseman (1952). The programme is based on the hypothesis that border-zone children are all about equally weak academically, and if they have other handicaps they are more likely to fail in the

[1] In parts of Germany, all candidates spend a fortnight or longer in the secondary school, and their ultimate admission depends on how they shape during this sample period. Probably the validity of this procedure could be very high; but it would hardly be practicable with the numbers involved in the British selection system.

grammar school. Those who are able to get on well with other children, who appear stable and sensible, who are constructive and effective in dealing with practical problems, are thought more likely to succeed in the grammar school than those who exhibit opposing traits. The procedure is based mainly on techniques developed by War Office Selection Boards, but also owes something to the experiments made by Dr Mary Clarke in selecting girls for admission to a direct-grant grammar school before the last war (Clarke, 1954). Since the introduction of the scheme for the border-zone in 1949 a good deal of trial and development has gone on, and it now contains three main elements:

(i) Observed activity. The children are given various outdoor tasks to do, working in groups of 10–14. The tasks are such things as erecting a tent, drawing a large plan of a fort on the playground, building things with assorted 'junk', making a 'bridge' with tubular scaffolding.
(ii) Observation of range of interests. The children are put into a classroom containing a large variety of different things: books; games; toys; material for drawing, painting, modelling, sewing, etc. They are given free scope to do whatever they wish. A fairly long period (45 minutes) is found to be necessary for full value.
(iii) Observation of lessons. The children are observed in a class while they are being taught two separate lessons. These are based on material which is likely to be new to the children, e.g. the idea of positive and negative numbers; codes; a first lesson in a foreign language, etc. Both oral and written answers to questions are used.

Each group of children has three observers, who make notes throughout the day and decide on an overall assessment at the end of it. No attempt is made to rate separate qualities such as intelligence or stability: the observer rates on the basis of 'grammar-school suitability'. Independent assessments are first made, and a final agreed assessment arrived at by discussion. The average correlation between observers approximates 0·80. The results have been followed up by comparing these border-zone accepts with others immediately above them in total test scores (who did not undergo the special procedure). No differences between the two groups were found after 18 months in the grammar school; but at 2½ and 3½ years there were fewer children assessed 'unsatisfactory' among the border-zone accepts. There appeared to be no differences in the numbers with high ratings for grammar-school success. This finding seems to support the rationale of the procedure, as outlined above. One major difficulty of the method, however, is that it is too elaborate and time-consuming to be readily applied to more than about two hundred children a year in a typical area.

In concluding this section, we may observe that there is a strong case for further experimentation along a number of lines, with good prospects of improving on the inflexible selection that results from employing purely objective, quantitative, procedures. But at the same time there is always the danger that the introduction of 'subjective hunches' may decrease the accuracy and fairness. Thus it is particularly necessary that such improvements should be introduced only under the supervision of someone with sufficient psychological and statistical training to ensure the inclusion of age allowances, to control as far as possible unreliability and variations between panels, interviewers or observers; and to plan and carry out adequate validation.

Turning now to the consideration of record cards and qualitative reports from the primary schools: let us first ask what factors —not covered by our present tests or by scaled estimates—should be allowed to have some weight in deciding on a pupil's suitability.

Variability. Children vary from day to day, even from hour to hour. Some are more nervous than others, or have been made over-anxious by their parents or teachers, so that their work under test conditions may be better or worse than usual. It is unfortunate, therefore, that under most Authorities, the crucial tests are often given all on a single day. We have already stated that an appreciable proportion would change their positions above, or below, the borderline were another similar examination—or even the identical one—given on another day.

This criticism is, however, apt to be exaggerated. As mentioned in Chapter VI, intelligence test results are not normally affected by mood or personal circumstances. Nevertheless this may occur among, perhaps, 1 or 2% of children, and it is possible (though not proven) that performance at attainments tests is more susceptible to such influences. The best way of allowing for these variations is to take account of primary-school marks or scaled teachers' estimates in selection. Increasing the thoroughness of the examination, and spreading it over a longer period, would also help. But we consider that, in addition, the primary heads should be encouraged to appeal on behalf of pupils who appear to have 'flopped' below their usual level, especially where some special circumstance (e.g. illness or recent death of a parent) may have upset them. This plan is already followed in some areas, and each year perhaps a dozen children enter grammar schools as a result.

Special Talents. The usual one-day examination cannot allow scope for the child with an intense interest in, and wide knowledge of, history, nature study, wireless, or a host of other specialities. Indeed the method of scoring the usual tests, giving equal weight to intelligence, English and Arithmetic, tends rather to favour good mediocrity at the expense of the unusually talented who are sometimes rather weak in, say, arithmetic or spelling.

Here again, those who have not studied the psychological facts are apt to over-estimate the defects of current selection procedure. For, as Terman has abundantly shown, talent and versatility tend to go together. The one-track mind among children is very much the exception. Nevertheless if the grammar school likes this type of child, as many good grammar schools do, such pupils should at least be brought to its notice. And it is hardly possible to express their suitability in any quantitative way.

Educational Opportunity. Variations in the type and the amount of schooling enjoyed by children are inevitable, and constitute one of the most difficult factors to evaluate and allow for. Many small rural schools, for example, are among the most delightful in the country, and may provide particularly valuable social and character training. But even with their smaller classes, the wide age range tends to make them less efficient, if judged by the children's level of attainments, than the large, streamed urban schools.[1] The intelligence test does something to redress the balance, but obviously the handicap remains where I.Q. + E.Q. + A.Q. constitutes the main basis of selection. The relation between conditions of schooling and attainment levels is so complex that no Authority, to our knowledge, has evolved any sound method of giving a quantitative bonus for such influences.

Discontinuity in a child's education is another very potent factor. Changes in staff in the middle of a school year, transfer at various ages from infant schools using varied methods, or even lack of consultation between the infant and junior departments of the same school, may produce temporary or lasting retardation. Particularly serious is the condition of those whose educational careers are characterized by a good deal of migration. Something like 10% of pupils may change residences within the U.K. between the ages of 5 and 10, and in addition there are quite a number who have spent part or most of their primary-school life in the Commonwealth or elsewhere abroad. The latter are often reported, by their present schools, to be making great strides in catching up with the English system; hence some allowance would seem to be specially desirable. Then there are the physically defective, and the unhealthy who have missed some key period of instruction. Apart from those officially classified as 'handicapped', there are many who pose problems that necessitate individual consideration: the hard of hearing or weak-sighted whose defects are not discovered till late in school life, others whose muscular control makes them poor and slow writers, and so on. All such considerations can, and should be, noted on the child's school record-card. But their effects can hardly be assessed other than subjectively.

Home Background. This is perhaps the most debatable item. Many would argue that the child who nearly reaches the conventional borderline, despite crowded conditions at home, financial anxiety,

[1] Evidence from the Kent Authority shows that the highest percentages of passes tend to be obtained by schools where the age-group lies between 30 and 40, or some multiple of this figure. Schools with much less than 30 are the least successful, but those between, say, 45 and 60 are also below average, presumably owing to difficulties of class organization. This would indicate that the poorer results of small schools are not attributable merely to lower intelligence in rural than in urban areas.

lack of culture, and even positive discouragement, should be rated higher than the child with but slightly better marks who has had every opportunity in a cultured home of making the best of his talents. Others would answer that there is a strong likelihood that the former will continue to be handicapped, and the latter helped, in the grammar school, hence our allocation would be improved if the allowance was given in the opposite direction. Since, however, the latter solution is obviously unacceptable in a democratic community, we would recommend that home backing should normally be disregarded, on the grounds of fairness. Any other solution would certainly fail to win the confidence of at least one section of the public. Yet at the same time, if the junior school can provide clear evidence that certain home circumstances are relevant (e.g. that there has been adverse strain in the past, but that the prospects of parental encouragement are good), then it should be possible to take this into account at the final stage of selection.

Parents' Wishes. It is obviously impossible to base allocation solely on parents' choice of school, not only because of the conditions to which attention was drawn in Chapter I, but also because the child's teachers and the district Education Officer are likely to have a fuller professional knowledge than the parents of the type of education for which the child is best fitted. Every effort should, of course, be made to meet any reasonable wishes, and it should be remembered that there are several considerations which parents are best able to assess. Apart from the relative prestige of the available schools, there are the relative conveniences of transport, past and present personal contacts, and children's already formed friendships. Again, the parents' vocational plans should certainly be paramount when there are several schools, at the same level, with different vocational biases to choose from.

While these considerations should, then, be taken into account by the junior-school head in drawing up his reports on children from his school, it is inevitable that—in most areas—many parents will be disappointed. Their wishes cannot normally be allowed to outweigh the indications of suitability obtained from tests and school estimates. Rather it should be the function of the junior school and the administration to keep parents thoroughly informed about the characteristics of the various secondary schools, so that they will not judge them merely on the basis of gossip, or on their own experience when they were at school; and thus to show them that the allocation of their child is decided as far as possible in the child's best interests. As suggested in Chapter IV, some Authorities have done admirable work in this field of public relations, but others are not sufficiently aware of its importance.

Panel Procedures. If it be agreed that individual children cannot and should not be fitted into neat mathematical pigeon-holes, and that a rigid system, however high its validity, may defeat its own ends, then we must try to suggest the most practicable and fair procedure for giving consideration to these largely non-quantifiable factors. Let us first distinguish five broad zones:

A. Pupils whose quantitative results are so high that all but 1 in 20 are likely to be successful in the grammar school. With a 20% entry, this means those with average quotients of 125 upwards (S.D. 15), or the best 5% of candidates. Corresponding figures can be calculated for other entry rates.

B. Pupils who are suitable with a fair degree of certainty, about three-quarters of them being likely to do well. They will have mean quotients of 116 to 124, and will include the next 9%.

C. The borderline group with 50–50 chances, namely the next 12% with quotients of 115 to 110.

D. Those with only about a 1 in 10 chance of succeeding, namely 24% with quotients of 109 to 100.

E. The almost certainly unsuitable 50%. Even the 90's to 99's have barely a 1 in 50 chance of success in the grammar school.[1]

A and E groups can be allocated with virtual certainty. But B, C and D constitute a border-zone group of 45%, which ranges from pupils about whom one is nearly certain that they should be admitted to grammar schools, through those about whom there is

[1] Note that, if we were able to select with complete accuracy from a, representative group of 100 children, we should pick up 4 to 5 of the A's 6–7 B's, 6 C's, 2–3 D's and 0–1 E's, that is the 20 in all for whom grammar-school provision is deemed appropriate. A validity coefficient of 0·90 for the quantitative data has been assumed in calculating these figures.

the greatest uncertainty, to those about whom it is nearly certain that they should not be allocated to grammar schools. Even though the B's will rarely if ever be rejected, and D's will seldom be accepted, it is desirable to consider every case individually and to judge whether non-quantifiable evidence can properly be taken into account. When allocations to technical schools have to be made at the same time, the situation is more complex, but in no way different in principle. Primary heads should now be informed as to which of their pupils fall into each zone, and should supply cumulative record cards for all B's, C's and D's, together with confidential reports on the C's and any B's or D's whose allocation they regard as questionable. In many cases the Education Officer in charge of selection will find the record-card indications, and even the parents' choices, consistent with the quantitative marks and he can forthwith reduce the border-zone group considerably at both ends. But the C's, together with occasional B's and more numerous D's where the head disagrees, or where other doubts exist (e.g. discrepancies between scaled estimates, if available, and tests) will still constitute a sizeable proportion, say 15%, of the age-group.

This reduced border-zone group should be considered by a panel consisting of primary, grammar and modern-school heads (not the primary heads directly concerned), an Education Officer, and, if possible, an educational psychologist. When scaled teachers' estimates are not available, the group can be summoned for additional examination, or for the application of any of the other procedures mentioned earlier in this chapter. The panel's task of studying each pupil's scores, record card and head's report is indeed an onerous, but not impossible, one. Thus for a catchment area of 450 pupils, supplying one 3-form entry grammar school, there would not normally be more than 70 pupils to consider, of whom some 30 would be passed. It would be for the Education Officer and psychologist to keep as tight a rein as possible on the use made of non-quantified evidence since—as indicated above, it is only in the exceptional case that subjective judgements should outweigh more objective data. The dangers of being influenced by chronological age should also be kept in the forefront.

A possible variant procedure, similar to that adopted in Wiltshire (cf. Chapter VIII), is for the panel to visit each primary school, and deal directly with the head, rather than through written reports. In the City of Lincoln, for example, the following information on all children in the top 40% is available to the panels: two I.Q.s and two sets of scaled school marks (obtained at 10+ and 11+), together with the school assessments of Industry, Health, Character and General Suitability, and remarks on special aptitudes and handicaps. In addition an independent report is made by a small interviewing panel, and the doubtful cases are further studied by visits to their schools. The border-zone pupils are followed up with especial care, and can be transferred to grammar or to modern school after each term in the first secondary year, or subsequently. This is perhaps the most thorough procedure we have met, and it is one which is acceptable to the teachers, and goes a long way to avoid strain on the children.

We have suggested that the Authority's educational psychologist should take part in the procedure. Actually psychologists have two roles, which should be distinguished. First they may act as assistants to the Chief Education Officer and—in this capacity—take responsibility for the tests or other methods adopted, for controlling the work of panels, etc. But secondly, psychologists with child-guidance training (including those employed under the National Health Service) may act as advisers to the panels, rather than as selectors. Their function is to examine children whose performance has been markedly irregular or contradictory, those who show signs of maladjustment, or those with minor physical handicaps which invalidate the ordinary procedure, and—taking account of home circumstances—to suggest the most suitable educational treatment. Obviously the number of children who can be so referred is strictly limited.

Conclusion. There is but little published information on the validity of such panel decisions, though individual children have often been followed up unsystematically in grammar schools. The most relevant investigation to date was carried out by Walker (1955) in Aberdeen, where the careers of 154 senior secondary-school entries were followed. Of these, 107 had passed the usual selection procedure, and 24 were borderline admits. Another 23 were below the borderline but were admitted after individual consideration of parents' or heads' appeals. The third group quickly surpassed the second; by the end of their third year they were doing as well on the average as the first group, and more of them were assessed by their teachers as suitable for fourth-year work.

Such favourable results might or might not hold good for panel schemes in general. Further inquiries are needed, and one would like to know how reliable or consistent are the judgements of parallel panels. Until fuller scientific support is forthcoming, it will be difficult to argue convincingly for the panel system against those Authorities which are satisfied either with purely quantitative, or with less well controlled qualitative, procedures.

X

Summary and Recommendations

CHAPTER I attempts to show that the problems of selection arise primarily from historical, administrative, political and social causes. Thus it is shortsighted to suppose that they could be solved merely by improving the various selection techniques, or abolishing intelligence tests, or the like. The development of the various complex strands of secondary education in England and Wales is outlined, and it is pointed out that these are very closely linked with the socio-economic class of the parents, despite considerable intermixing in recent years: the public boarding and foundation grammar and other independent schools with the upper middle classes, the maintained grammar schools with the 'white-collar' and upper working classes, and the secondary modern and unreorganized (all-age) schools with 'manual' classes. The parity of esteem envisaged in the 1944 Education Act is unlikely to be achieved so long as the curricula, vocational opportunities and social prestige of these schools are so widely differentiated. Hence instead of 'allocation by age, ability and aptitude' we are faced with highly competitive selection to grammar schools.

Recommendation 1. *Psychologists should realize—and should try to educate the public to understand—this wider background of selection, together with the conflicting social and political attitudes which largely underly its controversial features. As social scientists they should not feel committed to attack or to support the present system. Their function is to investigate those features which are psychologically beneficial or harmful to individual children, to the school and to society and, if they work for Local Authorities, to ensure that the procedures employed are the most appropriate and valid for the given set-up.*

CHAPTER II is mainly concerned to survey the administrative aspects of current selection, the procedures actually employed by the numerous Local Authorities, and their wide variations from one area to another. The history of, and reasons for, the introduction of intelligence and other objective tests, and statistical procedures, are briefly traced; and it is suggested that, in response to criticisms of recent years, there is a tendency to bring back more subjective and 'holistic' techniques, though at the same time paying more attention to their reliability and validity.

2. *Whatever may be the system of allocation or selection to different types of secondary education, the choice and application of the best methods of assessing children, and the correct treatment and interpretation of their results, are technically complex matters. Without in any way questioning the importance of the teachers' contribution, and of parents' wishes, we would insist that the procedures should be planned and supervised by persons with adequate psychological and statistical training.*

CHAPTER III discusses the broader sociological and psychological issues involved in the organization of secondary education. It is pointed out that the current—largely bipartite—system has greatly increased the opportunities for working-class children to obtain higher secondary education, though it still strongly favours middle-class children who do, in fact (with many individual exceptions) generally perform better academically and adjust more easily to the grammar-school milieu. The present bias of selection towards a linguistic-academic type of education, and the relative neglect of technical education, are open to criticism. But it is shown that common notions of contrasted types of children —the practical vs. the academic, or the leader vs. the intellectual —are psychologically misleading. Classification or streaming of pupils by different types of aptitude and interest is possible only to a limited extent at 11, and allocation must be based chiefly on general ability and all-round attainment. The arguments for and against any kind of streaming are examined; it is admitted that children's abilities are more variable than was earlier supposed, and that rigid streaming may have harmful educational and social consequences, though these are often exaggerated. In the light of these conclusions, various proposed alternative forms of secondary-school organization are discussed as impartially as possible, including the comprehensive school, common intermediate schools from 11 to 13, vocationally biased schools, etc. Since none of these is likely to be widely acceptable or practicable for some years to come, there would be advantages (though also disadvantages) in more frequent transfers after 11 years, particularly to the grammar school.

3. *Psychologists should frankly acknowledge that completely accurate classification of children, either by level or type of ability, is not possible at 11 years, still less on entry to the junior school at 7, and should therefore encourage any more flexible form of organization and grouping which gives scope for the gradual unfolding and the variability of children's abilities and interests. But they should also recognize the strong case for providing the brighter children with more advanced, and the duller ones with a simpler, kind of schooling; and should uphold their claim to be able to diagnose the most suitable form of schooling, for, not all, but a great majority of children.*

4. *In order to avoid unduly early and rigid segregation, either between different schools or within schools, we advocate the further development of individual and small-group work within classes, and the expansion of more diversified secondary courses, which would be as attractive to many parents as increased grammar-school provision.*

5. *Pupils whose proper allocation is in doubt should, wherever possible, be referred to an educational psychologist for individual diagnosis. This applies both to transfers to and from the grammar school in those areas where the current selection system continues to operate, and to streaming within comprehensive schools, or placement in technical or other vocationally biased courses, etc.*

6. *More research is needed in order to develop a wider range of aptitude, attainment and other tests as diagnostic tools for 12–16-year, as well as for 10–11-year pupils.*

CHAPTER IV tries to give a fair picture of the bad effects of selection on the mental health and personality development of children and on junior-school teaching, while also pointing out the exaggerations that often receive undue publicity. In general the emotional effects on children are probably less severe than the ill-feeling caused among parents, though the evidence does show that '11+ strain' may be a contributory factor in rare cases of maladjustment, delinquency or breakdown. The extent of direct and indirect parental pressure on children and their schools, and of coaching outside school hours (which mostly does more harm than good) is deplored. The distortion of the curriculum in many—by no means all—primary schools through preparation for the 11+ examinations affects not only its educational value, but also its contribution to the healthy emotional growth of children. The 'backwash effect' of objective intelligence and attainments tests is particularly undesirable, although much of the coaching that schools give in English and Arithmetic is, in fact, educationally useful. These effects, which naturally follow from the competitive nature of present-day selection, constitute the main reasons why most psychologists dislike the system, and look to the emergence of alternative types of school organization which would be based, instead, on the concepts of allocation and guidance.

7. *More attention should be paid to public relations by administrators, teachers and educational psychologists. Exaggerated statements in the press should be corrected, and publicity given to the full facts concerning national or local selection policies and procedures. Soundly-based criticisms from teachers and parents should be welcomed, and suggestions invited.*

8. *Through meetings of Parent-Teacher Associations and individual interviews, possibly also through leaflets and films, parents should be shown how to avoid inducing anxiety in their children, and the undesirability of out-of-school coaching.*

9. *Through discussions, e.g. at meetings of teachers' organizations, teachers themselves should try to clarify their attitudes to the selection examinations, to parental pressure, to coaching, etc., and to decide how best to eliminate harmful teaching practices.*

10. *More research is needed into 'old-type' and other forms of examination or assessment (including intelligence tests) which, without loss in predictive efficiency or undue unreliability in scoring, might have beneficial rather than harmful backwash effects.*

We would emphasize again that the problems of selection are largely determined by the current organization and administration of the secondary education system, and that therefore they may well change their complexion during the next 5 to 10 years. However, the second half of our Report assumes that selection will have to continue in most areas for some time to come. Thus CHAPTER V examines the evidence for its efficiency, under present conditions in predicting performance in secondary schools 1 or 2 years later, and up to School or General Certificate. The interpretation of this evidence is technically very complex, but it may be said that the usual combination of intelligence, English and Arithmetic tests reaches a very high degree of validity (the intelligence test being usually the best single predictor); and that when teachers' scaled estimates are also included, selection is about as accurate as it can be, in view of the natural alterations in interests and abilities as children grow older. Predictions of good or weak performance within the restricted grammar-school population are, as would be expected, less accurate. Even with a validity coefficient of 0·90, we would expect roughly one quarter of those accepted to do badly in the grammar school (when the entrance rate is 20%), and some 6% of those rejected to show equal or better achievement later. This accounts for the modern-school pupils who do well in G.C.E. and other apparently erroneous rejects, who in fact seem to amount only to some 3% of the total.

No definite answer can be given to the question—how far down in the scale of ability (as measured by standard tests) should we go in order to catch all those capable of advanced secondary schooling, since in practice such large variations are found between different schools in parental backing, in the traditions and interests of the schools and their teaching efficiency, and in policies regarding the G.C.E. Some successes in G.C.E. may well occur among pupils who are not even in the top 30% at 11 years; at the same time a considerable proportion of this top group are unsuited to an academic curriculum, and fail to complete the course.

11. *Practically all follow-up investigations have been conducted with a criterion of all-round intellectual achievement, or achievement in specific subjects. Research is needed into the broader*

aspects of 'benefiting from a grammar-school course', and their predictability.

12. *There is little to choose between the overall validities of various combinations of tests, examinations and estimates; but the intelligence test is so consistently successful that it should not be dispensed with (though it might be improved, cf. No.* 10).

13. *Relatively little gain in predictive efficiency can be expected from further 'tinkering with' most of the thorough selection procedures now in use. Rather we should consider them from the standpoint of their effects on the children, the schools, and public relations.*

14. *Even with these high validities, predictions can never approach perfection. Of pupils scoring in the top* 5%, *one in twenty are likely to prove failures in the average grammar school; and among pupils who score below the national average at* 11, *one in a hundred might turn out well if given the chance. Thus the border-zone, which receives special consideration before allocation is decided, should be considerably wider than is usual at present.*

15. *The inevitable imperfections even of highly valid predictions should be borne in mind in any plans for reorganizing the secondary educational system. It should also be realized that the proportion of the population suited to an academic course leading to good G.C.E. results is quite small (although needing to be drawn from a wide ability range); and that this proportion depends greatly on the quality of teaching in, and the 'morale' of, the particular school.*

CHAPTER VI describes the different kinds of intelligence tests, their scoring in terms of I.Q.s or standard scores, and their applicability to 11-year children. It is admittedly difficult to define what they measure, and although the factorial researches of Spearman, Burt, Thurstone, etc. help to clarify the problem, they do not pin down 'intelligence' as any one faculty. It is better regarded as all-round thinking abilities; and our ordinary verbal group tests provide a useful sampling of those thinking abilities needed for higher education; thus they are primarily tests of academic aptitude. A brief survey of the evidence relating to hereditary and environmental factors shows that such abilities, though deriving initially from a hypothetical innate capacity, are largely built up or acquired during childhood and adolescence, and are somewhat affected by the stimulating nature of the upbringing and the goodness of schooling. Yet though 'the I.Q.' fluctuates more widely during development than is generally supposed, it is sufficiently stable—say from 11 to 18 years—to allow useful predictions of educational capacity in the majority of children. Its correlation with the social class of the parents is also due partly to hereditary, partly to environmental factors; it is in any case so low that working-class parents produce larger total numbers (though smaller proportions) of very bright children. Group intelligence tests are admittedly susceptible to practice and coaching, but this does not invalidate their application at 11+, since the amount of improvement is limited, and a small amount of legalized practice produces as great an effect as intensive unauthorized coaching.

16. *It would be preferable to abandon the terms 'intelligence test' and 'I.Q.' in 11+ selection, and to substitute, e.g. 'general educability' or 'academic (or other) aptitude' tests. Psychologists should not claim that they are measuring purely innate ability, in contrast to acquired attainments.*

17. *The traditional system of scoring based on Mental Ages and I.Q.s is unsatisfactory, and all intelligence test scores for the normal range of ability should be converted to quotients (i.e. standard scores) with a Standard Deviation of 15. In general children should not be given I.Q. labels; the particular test and date must always be taken into account.*

18. *Group tests should be applied only by persons who have had appropriate training. More research is needed into the effects on group test results of the conditions of testing, the attitudes induced by the instructions, the effects of emotional strain, etc.*

19. *Coaching out of school, or in class, should be discouraged; but if it cannot be controlled, so that some schools, or some children, are gaining an advantage thereby, adequate previous practice and explanation in all schools should be authorized. In any case children should be familiar with the kind of test they are to take beforehand. Thereafter two tests should be given a few weeks apart, and their averaged result used as an important component in the selection procedure.*

20. *Further research is needed into the development of intellectual capacities in adolescence. Psychologists concerned in selection should try out new forms of prognostic tests and follow them up for several years (i.e. experimentally, not as part of the selection procedure itself).*

In CHAPTER VII, an historical survey of investigations of the marking of English essays brings out the great variations between markers, both in the averages and distributions of their marks, and in their rank orders. Variability in re-marking the same set of essays is almost as high, and there is little or no improvement when complicated analytic schemes are employed, rather than general impression. However at the 11+ selection stage, when the range of ability is wide, these personal errors can be largely overcome by combining the judgements of several markers. Perhaps more serious are variations between children's performance at different essay topics, showing that a single composition provides a very poor sample of their overall English ability. Nevertheless several recent follow-up studies indicate that the inclusion of an essay may improve the efficiency of prediction of secondary-school English, and many psychologists and teachers would agree that such inclusion would help to reduce backwash effects, and improve the basic qualifications of grammar-school entrants.

The development of objective or new-type tests of English and Arithmetic is shown to reflect, not merely the desire to measure more scientifically, but also changing views as to how these skills can best be taught. Despite improvements in recent years, they are still suspect among many teachers, and there is a case for the continued use of more conventional forms of examination, which have less backwash in that they more closely resemble normal school work. Provided these are constructed with due regard to these modern conceptions of teaching, and to likely sources of unreliability, they can give as good results in selection as the objective tests when combined with a standardized intelligence test.

21. *Although we generally favour the inclusion of an essay in selection examinations as an aid to the improvement of teaching,*

no weight should be attached to a single marking of a single composition by one of a group of examiners. At the very least, all pupils up for a particular grammar school should be marked by the same person; and it would be better to have 3 essays each marked by 3 persons if a really reliable score is desired. The marking can be done by quick impression methods and—to save time—can be largely confined to border-zone candidates. Running checks should be kept on the distributions, and consistency, of markers.

22. *It is not possible to reach a clear decision as to the superiority of old versus new-type attainments tests. They might with advantage be varied from year to year. But if old-type examinations are preferred, they should be constructed by persons with experience of psychometric techniques, tried out beforehand, and properly standardized on the test population.*

CHAPTER VIII shows that there is a strong case for using primary-school marks or teachers' estimates, both on the grounds of validity, and because they offer the possibility of eliminating written tests of attainment, with their attendant emotional stress, coaching and other backwash effects. The dangers of increased parental pressure should be recognized, but the main difficulty is the lack of comparability of standards from one school to another, which necessitates some form of quantitative scaling or standardization. Such scaling requires the application of an external test or tests to all schools, and reasonable accuracy is possible only if the tests are of high validity, and the groups from each primary school of fair size—say 30 upwards. A number of techniques of scaling are analysed here, and in Appendices C and D.

23. *Marks or estimates for pupils in small schools should not be employed in selection, except as part of a qualitative, border-zone procedure. For larger schools, the accuracy of selection will be increased by their inclusion, provided they are properly scaled. Subjective impressions of the standards of different schools are insufficient.*

24. *Marks or rank orders on particular subjects should be used rather than 'general suitability' or personality estimates; no particular subjects need be laid down.*

25. *The 'quota scheme' in its original form is not recommended. The estimates for all pupils should be scaled against an external test or battery either arithmetically (adjusting the mean and standard deviation, or the means of successive sub-groups), or perhaps more simply by smoothed percentile graphs. Age adjustments should be added to the scaled scores.*

26. *The external battery used for scaling must be as valid as possible, and should therefore include attainments tests or examinations as well as intelligence tests (though the former should receive less weight than the scaled estimates in actual selection). However, if it is particularly desired to eliminate attainments tests, the sum of two intelligence tests may be used—precautions having been taken against unequal coaching.*

27. *Possible alternatives, which dispense with testing at 11+, are the West Riding schemes for scaling against the junior schools' selection results in previous years, or—retrospectively—against their pupils' performance on tests given when they reach the secondary schools. The present trials of these schemes should be watched.*

CHAPTER IX shows that tests of spatial ability, and of mechanical and other interests can be of help in allocating children to technical schools. Personality qualities relevant to secondary-school success cannot be tested objectively, nor assessed satisfactorily by teachers—except in so far as they enter into primary-school attainments. Still less can they be judged in the ordinary selection interview, though some promising experiments with controlled interviews, and adaptations of group observational techniques, are described. In general, 'holistic' approaches, which try to bring together all relevant characteristics of the child, either by direct observation or from record-card data, are unlikely to be more valid than predictions derived merely from test scores and scaled estimates. Nevertheless they greatly improve the acceptability of the selection procedure, and may help to correct injustices among occasional pupils who 'flop' on one of the tests, or whose schooling has been irregular, or who show unusual talents, etc.

28. *We welcome the efforts being made by many Local Authorities to establish technical schools of equal quality with grammar schools, and consider that the same standards (at least in Intelligence and Arithmetic) should be required of their pupils as those demanded of grammar-school entrants. At the same time, further research by psychologists is needed on the development of tests for predicting success in technical, commercial, and other biased courses.*

29. *In areas with numerous small schools, where scaled teachers' estimates are not practicable, it is desirable to bring together all border-zone candidates for a given grammar school, and to apply a day's further examination, including specimen lessons and/or observation of group activities. Such procedures should be planned and supervised by a qualified psychologist or Education Officer. They should not include individual interviews, and their findings should be regarded as supplementary to, rather than superseding, the indications of the more objective tests.*

30. *Only among the top 5% or so and the bottom 50% (with a 20% acceptance rate) do we consider that allocation to grammar, technical and modern schools can be made automatically from test scores and scaled estimates. All intermediate pupils should be regarded as border-zone, and given special consideration by a panel of teachers, an Education Officer and/or an educational psychologist.*

31. *These panels should have available all the test results, etc., and the school record-cards or head's reports, but should not interview the children. The use made of this qualitative evidence in arriving at decisions should be carefully controlled, and checked by further follow-up research.*

32. *Record cards which provide cumulative data, including scores on successive sets of standardized tests, are of particular value, not merely as an aid in selection, but also for the educational guidance of children throughout their primary- and secondary-school careers.*

APPENDIX A

Follow-up Studies of the Validity of Selection

1. Extract from McClelland's (1942) Table XXXII.[1]

Predictive Value of Batteries for
Senior Secondary Schools

Battery	*Senior Secondary Schools*
IQ + Q + Ts	·804
IQ + Q + S + Ts	·800
Q + S + Ts	·790
IQ + Q	·786
Q + Ts	·783
IQ + Q + S	·783
IQ + S + Ts	·782
IQ + Ts	·779
Q+ S	·774
Q	·770
S + Ts	·764
IQ + S	·736
Ts	·720
S	·698
IQ	·691

IQ = Intelligence Quotient

Q = Qualifying examination (ordinary school examination)

Ts = Teacher's estimates

S = Standardized examination in English and arithmetic

[1] Reproduced by kind permission of the Scottish Council for Research in Education, and the University of London Press Limited.

2. Extract from Peel and Rutter's (1951) Table I.

Criterion composed of English Language, English Literature, French, Mathematics.

$n = 234$

	1944 Entrance Tests			*1949 School Certificate*			
	Intell.	*Eng.*	*Arith.*	*Eng. Lang.*	*Eng. Lit.*	*French*	*Maths.*
Entrance Tests:							
Intelligence		·62	·40	·48	·35	·43	·40
English			·21	·48	·46	·44	·17
Arithmetic				·13	·13	·21	·39
School Certificate:							
English Lang.					·54	·59	·37
English Lit.						·43	·33
French							·48
Mathematics							

Using as a criterion the four School Certificate subjects equally weighted, the total correlation of Intelligence, English and Arithmetic, equally weighted = 0·565. Multiple *r*, when the predictors are optimally weighted in the ratio 1, ·87, and ·27 = 0·585.

Note: these correlations were not corrected for selection.

3. Extract from Emmett and Wilmut's (1952) Tables IV and V. Correlations, Uncorrected for Selection, of 11+ Tests with Different S.C. Subjects.

S.C. Subject	*N*	Correlations with *I.Q.*	*E.Q.*	*A.Q.*
English Language	153	·505	·498	·204
English Literature	153	·296	·298	·266
History	153	·383	·336	·328
French	153	·451	·463	·359
Mathematics	153	·514	·299	·429
Physics	96	·401	·224	·319
Chemistry	105	·386	·254	·366
Latin	81	·443	·388	·396
Geography	139	·285	·101	·071
Biology	67	·124	·038	·046
Art	66	−·020	·115	−·048

Regression Weights for Maximum Prediction

Criterion	*Intelligence*	*English*	*Arithmetic*	r_m
English Language	·504	·432	−·171	·772
English Literature	·164	·261	·222	·620
History	·324	·153	·251	·701
French	·236	·380	·200	·785
Mathematics	·745	−·289	·330	·790
Physics	·694	−·289	·220	·638
Chemistry	·492	−·167	·340	·660

4. Extract from Emmett (1954).
Correlations and Optimum Weights for Twelve Grammar Schools ($n = 985$).

A. Using School Tests of Attainment

	1	2	3	4
1. Criterion	—	·792	·721	·735
2. Intelligence	·792	—	·853	·795
3. English	·721	·853	—	·695
4. Arithmetic	·735	·795	·695	—
Optimum Weights		·442	·149	·280
Multiple Correlation:	·814			

B. Using Standardized County Tests of Attainment

	1	2	3	4
1. Criterion	—	·786	·740	·768
2. Intelligence	·786	—	·803	·800
3. English	·740	·803	—	·720
4. Arithmetic	·768	·800	·720	—
Optimum Weights		·332	·232	·336
Multiple Correlation:	·831			

5. Extract from Richardson's (1956) Tables I and III.
Correlations of 'Old-Type' Attainments Tests, Moray House Intelligence, and Primary School Estimates with Achievement in Four Grammar Schools.

	1st Year *n* = *313*	*2nd Year* *n* = *286*
Qualifying Examination (Intelligence + English + Arithmetic)	·863	·846
Primary Estimates	·835	·791
Q.E. + Estimates	·865	·852
Intelligence + Estimates	·847	·834
Intelligence	·826	
English	·741	
Arithmetic	·792	
Arithmetic + English		·790
Arithmetic + English + Estimates		·827

Regression Weights for Maximum Prediction (Two Schools Only)

	1st Year *n* = *155*	*2nd Year* *n* = *145*
Primary Estimates	·535	·390
Intelligence	·110	·188
Proportion of Errors in Intelligence Test	·183	·231
English	·086	·047
Arithmetic	−·022	−·002
Multiple *r*	·850	·808

6. Extract from Peel and Armstrong (1956).

Prediction of Attainments at 11 grammar schools in English and Modern Language (equally weighted): multiple *r*'s for pairs of predictors, and regression coefficients for all three predictors.

EC = English Composition. MHE = Moray House English MHI = Intelligence

School	r_m EC+ MHI	r_m MHI+ MHE	r_m MHE+ EC	Regression Coefficients EC	Regression Coefficients MHE	Regression Coefficients MHI	r_m EC+ MHE + MHI
A	·62	·56	·53	·87	·54	1·00	·64
B	·60	·54	·53	·88	·37	1·00	·61
C	·47	·48	·45	·80	1·00	·80	·50
D	·66	·63	·66	1·00	·76	·52	·68
E	·44	·40	·38	·83	·31	1·00	·44
F	·39	·45	·43	·48	1·00	·62	·47
G	·49	·30	·44	1·00	·05	·55	·49
H	·56	·55	·54	·98	·87	1·00	·59
I	·63	·64	·55	1·00	·39	·20	·65
J	·69	·67	·59	·47	·33	1·00	·70
K	·45	·62	·63	·18	1·00	·03	·63

APPENDIX B

The Constancy of the I.Q.

A CRUCIAL consideration in the use of intelligence tests for educational prediction (guidance or selection) is the amount of variation likely to occur in a child's I.Q. for several years after he is tested. Though earlier claims for a rather high degree of constancy are now known to have been misleading, the reaction in the other direction may have gone too far. Dearborn & Rothney's (1941) illustrations of I.Q. variability are often cited, but they do not actually provide any usable information on its overall extent. Indeed it is difficult to find any investigation which satisfactorily answers the question—

How much variation should we expect when children are retested with a variety of standard tests either during the primary stage (say from 6 to 11 years), or in the secondary and early adult stages (say 11 to 15 or 20)?

The results of most studies are more or less distorted by one or more of the following factors:

(*a*) The similarity of the tests employed. Correlations between Terman-Merrill and a group test will be lower than between two similar group tests; verbal and non-verbal tests will also show lowered agreement.

(*b*) The time interval. The size of correlations probably drops off more rapidly at first, say from 1 week to 1 year, then more slowly up to 3–4 years, then little further change up to 10 years.

(*c*) Age at first testing. Tests much before 5 are known to have little predictive value, and variations from 6 to 11 are at least as great as from 11 to 20.

(*d*) The range of ability in the group. Correlations (though not necessarily the mean size of variations) are lowered in groups of restricted range.

(*e*) The level of ability of the group. Terman and Merrill's results show 1·12 times larger variations around I.Q. 120 than in a representative group, 0·88 smaller at I.Q. 80.

(*f*) The S.D. of I.Q.s in a representative sample. Terman-Merrill at 12 years with a S.D. of 20 will naturally show high variability. Indeed our question above cannot be answered unless we agree on some standard value, say 15.

(*g*) The reliability of the tests compared. We shall only be talking of tests that can be assumed to have a short-period retest (or parallel form) reliability of ·90 or over in a representative group. We shall assume also that the tests have been properly given, so that reliability is not reduced by defective conditions or bad scoring.

(*h*) If several tests are applied, each individual's maximum range of variation is larger than when two tests only are compared. Published data appear to confirm the supposition that the P.E. of the former (i.e. the median variation) is:

$$2 \times \cdot 6745\, \sigma\sqrt{1 - r} \text{ and of the latter: } \cdot 6745\, \sigma\sqrt{1 - r^2}$$

Thus the former is usually about $1\frac{1}{2}$ times the latter.

(*i*) If the norms for the second test are 'x' points more generous all-round than those for the first test, the main effect will be to produce more gains than losses of score. But it will also raise the median variation (regardless of sign), by:

$$\sqrt{1 + \frac{\cdot 6745^2 x^2}{\text{P.E.}^2}}$$

Thus a small difference in norms, say 4 points, would raise a median variation of 8 only to 8·5; but with bigger differences the effect rises disproportionately. Similar effects will occur if some or all of the testees have been more coached or practised on one test than another.

(*j*) No account is taken here of differential effects attributable

N

to gross environmental changes, such as those claimed by Wellman, Schmidt, A. D. B. Clarke, etc. We are referring only to normal variations in British or North American cultures.

We may now consider the published findings. Thorndike (1933) surveyed 36 correlations, mainly from Stanford-Binet given twice over various intervals, and concluded that the correlation fell regularly from 0·89 at 0 months to 0·70 at 5 years. No account was taken of points (*c*), (*d*), (*e*) or (*i*), so this tells us practically nothing. His figures are, of course, raised by (*a*), as identical tests only were compared.

Hirsch (1930) tested children (mostly aged 7 to begin with) at roughly yearly intervals with 3 versions of Otis Primary and 3 of Otis Advanced. Miller (1933) picked out the results of 160 who completed all these tests and converted all I.Q.s to the same mean (103) and S.D. (14·6), thus eliminating factors (*f*) and (*i*). The lowest correlation was 0·76 (actually the 3rd with the 6th year, not the first with the 6th). This corresponds to a P.E. of 6.6, and accords reasonably with the obtained median variation (from Test 1 to Test 6) of 7·3. The maximum variations over all 6 tests ranged up to 36, and suggest a median of about 9. This accords well with our expectation under (*h*). Since the first three tests are non-verbal, the last three verbal, the degree of similarity (*a*) is only moderate. Thus this result seems to be a particularly trustworthy one, not seriously distorted by any of the factors mentioned.

Perhaps the most satisfactory study to date is Husen's (1950) testing of all the children in a Swedish town with a verbal test battery at 9½, and the retest of nearly the whole male group (722) on call-up at 19½, with a similar (though not parallel) verbal and non-verbal battery. His correlation was 0·72.

Burt (1954) claims a correlation of 0·84 for 782 cases tested at 10–12 with a group test (supplemented by individual) and a retest 8 to 13 years later. The tests were rather closely parallel, and their reliability was increased by supplementary individual testing of cases whose original results were queried by teachers. Thus this correlation is somewhat higher than those obtained in any other study except, possibly, Honzik's (where 8-year Terman-Merrill correlated 0·83 with 14–15-year Terman-Merrill in a restricted and above average sample).

Honzik et al's (1948) statement that, over 6–18 years, 58% of some 150 to 200 testees varied 15 or more I.Q. points, is often quoted. A P.E. of, say, 16, is of course an impossibility under normal conditions; even if the correlation between the first and last test was zero, it would only be $\cdot 6745 \times 15 = 10\cdot 1$. Probably (though this is not made clear) it refers to raw I.Q.s which, in the case of Terman-Merrill, have an unduly high S.D. at most age levels. Fortunately we are also told that 5 cases, say $2\frac{1}{2}\%$, showed changes of $2\frac{1}{2}\sigma$ and over; this gives us a P.E. of 12·5, not 16. This figure represents maximum variations over 8 or more tests; if we compared one pair of tests only, it would drop to about 9.3. Even this is exaggerated, since the mean I.Q. of the group was around 120, and, with so many tests, practice effects must have entered to some extent. We may conclude then that true variations from 6 to 18 have a median of about 8 points, and this corresponds precisely with the obtained correlation of 0·61. Thus, when we allow for factors (*e*), (*f*), (*h*) and (*i*), Honzik's results accord closely with those of other workers.

Now his correlation for Stanford-Binet at 6 years with Terman-Merrill at 11 is approximately 0·71, and for Terman-Merrill at 11 with Wechsler-Bellevue at 18 is about 0·75. These coefficients may be too low because the group's range of ability was somewhat restricted (factor *d*); on the other hand they are high because of (*a*)—the rather close similarity of the tests. Possibly we can regard these influences as balancing out, and therefore conclude that 0·70 represents about the lowest correlation to be expected over these age ranges between moderately similar tests. The same conclusion is indicated by Miller's and Husen's results. Thus the P.E. for a single retest is 7·2 and for a large number of retests the median maximum variation is 9 to 10 points.

In actual practice, however, factors such as (*e*), (*f*) and (*i*) often distort the results and produce apparently greater variations. Comparisons of wholly non-verbal, or performance, tests with verbal (individual or group) tests would also yield larger fluctuations. The distribution of variations corresponding to P.E.s of

7·2 and 10·1 are shown in the last two columns of the Table below. The earlier columns show variations for r's of 0·90 and 0·80 such as might be expected for identical tests over intervals of 1 month and 5 years respectively.

Gains or Losses in I.Q. Points	*One pair of Tests*			*Several Tests*
	r = 0·90 P.E. 4·5	r = 0·80 P.E. 6·1	r = 0·70 P.E. 7·2	r = 0·70 P.E. 10·1
40+				0·7 %
30–39		0·1 %	0·6 %	3·9
20–29	0·3 %	2·9	6·0	14·2
15–19	2·4	7·5	10·8	14·0
10–14	12·2	18·4	20·0	19·4
5–9	33·8	32·9	30·0	23·8
0–4	51·4	38·2	32·6	24·0

APPENDIX C

The Reliability of Scaling of Primary School Marks and Estimates

TEACHERS' MARKS and assessments may be unreliable in the sense that two or more teachers assessing the same children may differ both in their overall standards and in their orders of merit. Here, however, we are concerned with the trustworthiness of the scaling process. If an intelligence test (or a battery of tests) shows that 20% of the candidates from one school fall above a given borderline, the 20% with the highest school rankings then being selected, we need to ask whether another similar test or battery would yield a figure of 20%, or whether it might vary by 1, 2, 5, or 10% or more. In the 1949 N.U.T. Report, Dr. Jeffery analysed the probable size of the quota yielded by a second test, but did not deal with this liability to variation. Alternatively, scaling may be based on the mean and S.D. of a group of candidates. Thus if the children from a typical school score 100 on the first test or battery, and the averaged teachers' estimate is converted to this figure, how widely might the mean score vary on another test?

Now if a school submitted a single candidate, then the S.E. of his score on another test correlating r with the first would be: $\sigma\sqrt{1-r^2}$. (Note that it is more appropriate to use this formula than: $\sigma\sqrt{1-r}$, since the latter indicates the extent of variation of the candidate's first score from his hypothetical true score given by a completely reliable test.) With n candidates, the S.E. of their mean score on the second test will be: $\dfrac{\sigma\sqrt{1-r^2}}{\sqrt{n}}$

However, when scaling is based on quotas, or other techniques involving percentages of pupils, the S.E. will be increased by:

$$\frac{2{\cdot}0566\, z_{50} pq}{z_p}$$

where p is the percentile at which the borderline is drawn and z_{50} and z_p the normal curve ordinates at the median and at the required percentile. At the 80th percentile, this ratio$=1{\cdot}429$.

For illustration, let us take a one-stream school with $n=40$, a mean I.Q. of 100 at the first test, and $\sigma=15$. Naturally the mean and variance on the first test will differ considerably from one school to another, but we can get an idea of the sort of reliability to expect by employing average figures. For specimen values of r we will take 0·95, 0·90 and 0·75. We then find that the Standard Errors are as follows:

r	*S.E.* *mean*	*S.E* *80th percentile*
0·95	0·739	1·057 I.Q. or E.Q. points
0·90	1·033	1·478
0·75	1·567	2·238

The most probable or median variation on retest will be 0·6745 times these figures, and the 1% confidence limits (likely to be exceeded only once in 100 schools) will be 2·58 times larger.

Let us translate these figures into the proportions likely to score above a borderline which initially selects the best 20% of candidates. This borderline falls at $0{\cdot}842\sigma$ above the mean, according to Normal Curve Tables, i.e. at a quotient of 112·63. Now suppose that our school scores at its second test a mean of $100 + 2{\cdot}58 \times 0{\cdot}739 = 101{\cdot}91$, or $100 - 2{\cdot}58 \times 0{\cdot}739 = 98{\cdot}09$. The fixed borderline quotient then falls at 10·72 and 14·54 points above these new means. Referring again to Normal Curve Tables, we find that 23·7% of the group with the raised mean will score above the borderline; but 16·6% of the group with the lowered mean will score above it. The other entries in the following Table are calculated similarly:

(*i*) *R*	(*ii*) *P.E.* (*mean*) %	(*iii*) *P.E.* (*quota*) %	(*iv*) 1 % *Limits* (*mean*) %	(*v*) 1 % *Limit* (*quota*) %
0·95	1·0	1·4	16·6–23·7	15·3–25·4
0·90	1·3	1·9	15·4–25·3	13·7–27·8
0·75	1·9	2·8	13·3–28·4	11·0–32·4

Col. (*ii*) shows the median variation when scaling is based on the mean test score of the group, and (*iii*) the median variation when based on the quota system. The ·01 limits of variation according to the two systems are similarly shown in Cols. (*iv*) and (*v*). Thus on the quota system, when the correlation of the first test or battery with a slightly different one is, say 0·90, the original quota of 8 out of 40 may alter on the second test to anywhere between 5·5 and 11·1, although the median alteration will be only $\pm$ 0·76 individuals.

For a smaller school with, say, 10 candidates the limits of variation will be roughly twice as big; whereas for a school with 160 candidates they will be halved. All these figures, however, refer to percentage variations. In terms of actual numbers the variations for smaller schools may not appear quite so serious, as illustrated by the following Table:

	Size of Age Group	*Expected Quota*	*Median Variation of Quota*	*1 % Limits of Variation*
r=0·90	10	2	0·38	0·7 to 3·6
	40	8	0·76	5·5 to 11·1
	160	32	1·52	27·0 to 38·2

Since the above calculations are based on somewhat complex statistical arguments, it seemed desirable to obtain an empirical check. Two sets of quotients for 400 boys, correlating 0·87 with one another, were taken. The boys were split at random into groups of 40, and then again into groups of 10. In each group the top 20% on Test 1 were picked out and the cutting quotient or borderline was noted. The numbers with quotients at or above this figure in the same group on Test 2 were then counted. In the groups of 40, with a quota of 8, the actual range on Test 2 was from 5 to 11. In the groups of 10, the range was from 0 to 4. Considering the small total numbers, these figures agree quite well with the theoretical predictions.

These same figures can be used to answer another somewhat different question. Suppose that it were possible to establish the correct quota for a particular junior school as 20%, e.g. by following up its selectees in secondary schools, then what variation from this true figure would be expected when the estimates are scaled on various tests? The answer is given by the same Tables. If we take 0·90 as the validity of the battery used for scaling, and apply an accurate scaling technique, then the limits of error are 15·4 to 25·3%. That is, in a school which really deserved to get 8 places, the scaling process may assign it anywhere from 6·2 to 10·1 places. But if we adopt the quota system and scale on one intelligence test with a validity of only 0·75, the obtained quota will show much more serious variations, ranging from 4·4 to 13·0.

This finding is clearly relevant to the problem discussed by McClelland (1942) as to whether scaling of English and Arithmetic estimates should be based, (*a*) on separate English and Arithmetic tests, (*b*) on a combined attainment test score, (*c*) on an intelligence test. He concludes that the accuracy of (*b*) is less than that of (*a*), and that (*c*) is too inaccurate a technique to be considered. Now his criterion was the approximation of mean school scaled estimates to the mean school attainment scores, hence naturally (*a*) met this criterion the best. But the proper criterion is the approximation of the mean school scaled estimate to the mean performance of that schools' pupils in secondary work; and this, in our view, will depend on the correlation of the scaling instrument with the follow-up data, not on the correlation of the estimates with the scaling instrument. Thus considerably more accurate scaling will be obtained from a battery of intelligence and attainments tests (with a validity of around 0·90) than from single tests (with validities around 0·75).

Three points should be made finally. First, this discussion has no bearing on whether the right pupils are selected, only on the selection of the right *numbers* from each school. Despite the unreliability that we have pointed out, the evidence that the use of estimates tends to help in picking out the most able still stands. Secondly, precisely the same unreliability applies to selection based on tests, not on estimates at all. If a single intelligence, or attainments, test were used, the numbers of places gained by small schools would show enormous chance variations. Hence it is essential to aim at a battery with the highest possible validity, whether or not estimates are taken into consideration. Thirdly it should be realized that, however great may be the unreliability of quotas derived from estimates and tests, the variability of teachers' standards is likely to be greater still. Unfortunately no comparative figures are available. But if we take McClelland's results (quoted in Chapter VIII) as typical, they suggest that the likely error in a teacher's estimate of the average ability of his class is just about twice the error of an estimate based on an intelligence test with a validity of 0·75. For example, with a 'true' quota of 8, the class teacher's or head's estimates might in extreme cases range from about 3 to 15. We may conclude then that even inaccurate scaling is far better than no scaling at all.

APPENDIX D

Specimen Techniques of Scaling

1. *Rank Order Conversions.* The simplest technique is that adopted by the National Foundation for Educational Research in its earlier (unpublished) investigations with the Middlesex Education Authority. The primary-school head provides a list of the children in his age-group in order of merit for grammar-school suitability, based in any way he wishes on school marks or teachers' judgements. A separate list of I.Q.s on the Authority's examination is obtained. Then the child with the highest school rank is assigned a quotient identical with the highest I.Q. in that school; the second on the school's list is given the next highest quotient, and so on. Finally these quotients for the school order and the children's *own* intelligence quotients can be combined with any desired weighting.

An obvious objection is that, with a small group, an irregular distribution of I.Q.s may give an inaccurate picture of the distribution of attainments. For example the group might obtain I.Q.s of 130, 128, and then the rest in a bunch around 100 to 80. But the two children with the highest school rankings might not be considered by the school as being actually much ahead of the 3rd and 4th on the list.

Another defect is that the technique, as described here, does not make age allowances; and there is no easy way of applying such adjustments to rank orders. However this could be overcome by scaling the rank positions against intelligence test scores, and then converting each child's scaled school score to a quotient by reading off from his score and age in the I.Q. Table issued with the test.

If a battery is used for scaling, say intelligence, English and Arithmetic, it is probably simpler to take I.Q. + E.Q. + A.Q., rather than combined scores. But then the resulting scaled quotients will need to be re-corrected for age by one of the standard procedures (cf. Lawley, 1950).

2. *Percentile Graphs.* The reliability of scaling for smallish groups is likely to be improved by the following technique. A graph is drawn for each school, the highest mark or rating being plotted against the highest I.Q. (or test score or battery total), then the next highest against the next, and so on. When the number of cases exceeds 20 or so it will suffice to plot every alternate, or every third, etc., case in the middle range. For still larger numbers, the 99th, 95th, 90th, 75th, 50th, etc., percentiles for the estimates and the test may be plotted. A smoothed line or curve is then drawn by eye, and the scaled score read off for each estimate. Here, if the top three children have been awarded estimated marks of, say, 90, 80 and 78, the scaled scores will more nearly reflect the intervals between them instead of, as in No. (1) depending on the intervals that happen to occur between the I.Q.s or test scores.

3. *Sutcliffe and Canham's Technique.* An alternative technique, likely to yield very similar results, is described by Sutcliffe and Canham (1944). The ratings or estimates and the external test marks of the group are ranked separately, and each divided into five equal (or nearly equal) sections: e.g. Nos. 1–5, 6–10, . . . 21–25. The mean of the top section of ratings is plotted against the mean of the top section of scores, and so on, and a smoothed conversion line drawn and extrapolated. This method would be suitable with groups down, to, say, 15; for groups larger than 40–45, it might be preferable to increase the number of sections, and the points on the graph.

In Lincoln, at present, the summed school ranks for Arithmetic Accuracy, Arithmetic Problems, English Usage and English Comprehension + Expression are scaled in this way against I.Q. both at 10+ and at 11+. There are no school examinations or other signs of selection for the class teachers or pupils to worry about. Further detailed consideration is given to border-zone pupils (cf. Chapter IX).

4. *Equating Means and Standard Deviations.* A good example of this technique was devised by Edwards (1951) for the Wigan Authority. For each school is calculated the mean and S.D. of

internal assessments of English ability, and of scores on an objective English Test. A simple graph is drawn for converting the former to the same scale as the latter, namely a straight line running through the two points 1σ above and 1σ below the mean on each variable. The scaled estimates are then converted to quotients by means of a table which provides age allowances. Similarly, Arithmetic assessments are scaled against an Arithmetic Test. These four quotients, together with I.Q.s from two tests, are plotted on a 'psychograph' for each child, and this is open to inspection by his parents and teachers. Normally a mean (rescaled) quotient of 115 or over is required for grammar-school admission, but special consideration is given to certain cases, such as those showing an unexpected 'flop' on one of the six measures.

In the light of Appendix C, this particular system is probably less reliable than scaling based on combined attainments and intelligence tests. Another weakness is that although conversions based on means and sigmas are theoretically more reliable than those using percentiles, inaccuracies may occur if either distribution is skewed. This is particularly likely to occur when, as in some areas, only the top half or so of the population is considered for selection. Thus Method (2) seems preferable, and is in addition quicker and simpler.

5. *Northumberland County Authority* (Bosomworth, 1953). In Northumberland, more weight is given to a child's scaled 'T' score than to any other single measure. Primary-school heads are asked to place their candidates in order of merit on the basis of their normal day-to-day school work in Oral and Written English, Mental and Written Arithmetic, Nature Study and Social Studies. These six orders are converted to 'T' scores (mean 50, standard deviation 10), and a child's average 'T' score is taken as a measure of his work in the primary school. The scores are then scaled so that their mean becomes equivalent to the mean total score of the class or school on the external Grading Examination (intelligence + attainments); finally adjustments are made for age. Other features of the system are that attainments tests are given at 7+, which help the primary-school heads to realize how their schools compare with others. A system of area panels

copes with borderline cases, and the information gathered at these meetings is made available to the primary heads. Lastly, the heads are kept informed about the later progress of their pupils in grammar and in modern schools.

6. *McIntosh's Technique* (1952). This technique was developed particularly for scaling estimates of very small groups, say 6 to 12 candidates. For each group, the estimate of each pupil's ability in English is plotted against *his own* English test score, and the best fitting regression line is drawn by eye through the mean of the estimates and the mean of the scores. If the estimates are weak ones, no relation is likely to be apparent in the graph, and they are then disregarded for this school. Occasional pupils who appear to have 'flopped' on the test can be disregarded in drawing the graph, but yet be given scaled scores corresponding to their estimates. Similarly, Arithmetic estimates are scaled against Arithmetic test scores.

A possible weakness is that the variance of the scaled estimates will be reduced below that of the scores by an amount depending on the lowness of correlation between them. Under the conditions of selection in England, it would be inconvenient to have to deal with scaled estimates whose range varied in this way from one school to another.

7. *Sandon's Technique* (1956). Sandon appears to be one of the few investigators to have realized that discrepancies between mean school estimates and mean objective test scores arise partly through variations in standards of judgement and partly through chance fluctuations such as we have discussed in Appendix C. (He points out that estimates may also vary from school to school in their dispersion and in their correlations with test scores, but —in the example he quotes—to a barely significant extent.) Now it is only the former type of discrepancy that needs to be corrected in scaling. He therefore draws a single regression line from the estimates and scores of all schools, and indicates by parallel lines above and below this line what mean estimate (for a school of given size) deviates significantly from the value to be expected from the mean score. When the mean school estimate falls within these chance limits, the schools' estimates are accepted as they stand. But for other schools an appropriate

amount is added to, or subtracted from, the estimates for all pupils.

Interesting as is this treatment of the problem, it cannot, of course, really determine how much of any discrepancy represents chance error, how much false judgement. We would prefer to put less trust, rather than more, in estimates from schools which have so few pupils that their inaccuracy cannot be proven.

8. *Bradford Education Authority.* Two intelligence tests are given and each school provides A–E ratings of its pupils under six headings; the latter are summed to yield scores ranging from −12 to +12, and multiplied by 3 to yield a scale roughly comparable to an I.Q. scale. A panel compares these scores with the test results, 'and in any case where there is a serious discrepancy in means, spread or order the school is asked to reconsider and, at discretion, to revise its assessments. It is hoped that the number of schools where this revision proves necessary will rapidly diminish with experience'. This is not very different, in effect, from the quota scheme, though less formal. It may be somewhat more reliable than the quota scheme, despite the element of subjective judgement in the panel's decisions regarding 'serious discrepancy'. Conceivably it would work well in a circumscribed area where all the primary schools are of fair size.

9. *Scaling against Follow-up Criteria.* In unpublished memoranda, G. F. Peaker has suggested methods of dispensing with tests at the time of selection, and scaling each primary school's estimates or marks against results obtained later by that school's pupils in the secondary school. For example, a grammar school with an entry of 90 pupils would rank them at the end of the first year for all-round achievement. If primary school A has provided 10 of these pupils, and their average rank was close to 45½, it could infer that it was recommending candidates of just about the right calibre. If, however, their mean rank was 36, it had probably been too strict, and could be more generous in its recommendations next year; whereas if the mean was 55, it had probably been too lenient. A fair amount of variation from year to year would, of course, be expected by chance; hence only fairly large deviations from 45½ are likely to be significant. Peaker has indicated that the 'tolerance limits' in this instance

might be between 37 and 55. Presumably the numbers from each primary school entering any given grammar school must be fairly large, probably 10 or more, otherwise the 'tolerance limits' would be so wide as to offer little guidance.

Clearly the plan is an attractive one in that schools which over-estimated their pupils' capabilities, or which had amassed an undue share of places through coaching, would be shown up; whereas those which provided the best preparation for grammar-school work would reap their reward. The obvious difficulty is that the follow-up information must be retrospective; for example, if the 1955 selectees from a particular primary school turned out poorly, allowance could hardly be made for this until the time came for it to recommend its 1957 pupils. Furthermore, it is known that both age and social class affect success in the grammar school. Hence primary schools which (contrary to present practice) made most allowance for these factors in their recommendations would achieve the best follow-up results, while those which recommended younger working-class children would be less successful.

Another method, which is about to be tried out as a shadow scheme on a large scale, avoids the last criticism, and has the advantage of being based on all pupils, not on grammar entrants only. It too eliminates all external tests in the primary school and thus, effectively, 'abolishes the 11+'. Instead, all pupils take standardized tests at their secondary schools in the following November, and the (previously awarded) estimates or marks from each junior school are scaled against these results. The conversion tables thus prepared will be used for calibrating the marks given by the schools to their next year's candidates. (A technique of scaling is also proposed, similar to that of Sutcliffe and Canham—No. 3 above—but involving only simple self-checking arithmetic, not graphs.) An essential part of the plan is that, while each junior school can prepare its marks in any way it thinks best, using what components it likes, several years will be allowed for it to stabilize its system and to gain experience in holding its own standards sufficiently constant from year to year. This will be demonstrated if the retrospective re-scalings necessitate only slight alterations in that school's conversion table. Eventually, then, selection can be based on the junior school's scaled marks only, though any of the usual border-zone procedures can be added for doubtful candidates from all schools.

We foresee considerable complexities in collecting the secondary stage test scores for each primary school and preparing its revised conversion table; and the author admits that fluctuations in standards may be too great for the scheme to be workable. But we certainly look forward with interest to the results of the trials.

In conclusion: each of these schemes has its merits, and may well be appropriate to particular local conditions. Method 2 would appear to be as technically sound as any, and the simplest to apply both in urban and in more scattered areas.

Bibliography

ALEXANDER, W. P. (1935): Intelligence, Concrete and Abstract. *Brit. J. Psychol. Monogr. Suppl.*, No. 19.

BENE, E. (1955): *A Study of Some Aspects of A. Davis's Theory of Socialized Adaptive Anxiety*. Ph.D. Thesis, University of London.

BIRCH, L. B. (1955): The Incidence of Nail Biting among School Children. *Brit. J. Educ. Psychol.*, 25, 123–8.

BLANDFORD, J. S. (1957): *Standardized Tests in the Junior School with Special Reference to the Effects of Streaming on the Constancy of the Results*. M.A. Thesis, University of London.

BOARD OF EDUCATION (1920): *Report of the Departmental Committee on Scholarships and Free Places*. London: H.M.S.O.

BOARD OF EDUCATION (1924): *Report of the Consultative Committee on Psychological Tests of Educable Capacity*. London: H.M.S.O.

BOARD OF EDUCATION (1928): *Free Place Examinations*. Pamphlet No. 63. London: H.M.S.O.

BOARD OF EDUCATION (1931): *Report of the Consultative Committee on the Primary School* (Hadow Report). London: H.M.S.O.

BOARD OF EDUCATION (1938): *Report of the Consultative Committee on Secondary Education* (Spens Report). London: H.M.S.O.

BOARD OF EDUCATION (1943): *Report of a Committee of the Secondary Schools Examinations Council on Curriculum and Examinations in Secondary Schools* (Norwood Report). London: H.M.S.O.

BOSOMWORTH, G. (1953): The Use of Teachers Assessments in Allocating Children to Secondary Schools. *Durham Res. Rev.*, 4, 50–53.

BOYD, W. (1924): *Measuring Devices in Composition, Spelling and Arithmetic*. London: Harrap.

BURT, C. L. (1921): *Mental and Scholastic Tests*. London: King.

BURT, C. L. (1943a): Validating Tests for Personnel Selection. *Brit. J. Psychol.*, 34, 1–19

BURT, C. L. (1943b): Ability and Income. *Brit. J. Educ. Psychol.*, 13, 83–98.

BURT, C. L. (1943c): The Education of the Young Adolescent: Psychological Implications of the Norwood Report. *Brit. J. Educ. Psychol.*, 13, 126–40.

BURT, C. L. (1947): Symposium on the Selection of Pupils for Different Types of Secondary Schools. I. A General Survey. *Brit. J. Educ. Psychol.*, 17, 57–71.

BURT, C. L. (1954): Age, Ability and Aptitude. Univ. London Inst. Educ. Stud. Educ., No. 6. *The Problems of Secondary Education Today*. London: Evans.

CAMPBELL, W. J. (1952): The Influence of Home Environment on the Educational Progress of Selective Secondary School Children. *Brit. J. Educ. Psychol.*, 22, 89–100.

CARR, J. W. (1957): *The Value of Procedures Supplementary to the Standard Tests in Secondary School Selection*. M.A. Thesis, University of London.

CAST, B. M. D. (1939–40): The Efficiency of Different Methods of Marking English Composition. *Brit. J. Educ. Psychol.*, 9, 257–69; 10, 49–60.

CLARK, H. (1956): The Effect of a Candidate's Age upon Teachers' Estimates and upon his Chances of Gaining a Grammar School Place. *Brit. J. Educ. Psychol.*, 26, 207–17.

CLARKE, A. D. B. and CLARKE, A. M. (1954): Cognitive Changes in the Feebleminded. *Brit. J. Psychol.*, 45, 173–9.

CLARKE, M. G. (1954): Grammar School Selection: A Successful Experiment in Group Interviews. *Times Educ. Suppl.*, 26th March.

CLEGG, A. B. (1953): Some Problems of Administration in West Riding Grammar Schools. *Univ. Leeds Res. & Stud. Educ.*, 7 7–15.

COLLINS, M. (1954–5): The Causes of Premature Leaving from Grammar Schools. *Brit. J. Educ. Psychol.*, 24, 129–42; 25, 23–35.

CONNOR, D. V. (1952): *The Effect of Temperamental Traits upon Intelligence Test Performance*. Ph.D Thesis, University of London.

DANIELS, J. C. (1955): Letter to *Times Educ. Suppl.*, 29th July.

DAVIDSON, M.A. *et al.* (1957): The Distribution of Personality Traits in Seven-Year-Old Children. *Brit. J. Educ. Psychol.* 27.

DAVIS, D. RUSSELL and KENT, N. (1955): Intellectual Development in School Children, with Special Reference to Family Background. *Proc. Roy. Soc. Med.*, 48, 993–5.

DEARBORN, W. F. and ROTHNEY, J. W. M. (1941): *Predicting the Child's Development*. Cambridge, Mass.: Sci-Art.

DEMPSTER, J. J. B. (1954): *Selection for Secondary Education*. London: Methuen.

DEMPSTER, J. J. B. (1955): Modern Pupils Assessed: Exam Results at 'O' Level. *Times Educ. Suppl.*, 4th Nov.

DREW, L. L. (1946): A Selection Technique for Pre-Apprenticeship Courses. *Occup. Psychol.*, 20, 34–43.

EDGEWORTH, F. V. (1888): The Statistics of Examinations. *J. Roy. Stat. Soc.*, 51, 599–635.

EDGEWORTH, F. V. (1890): The Element of Chance in Competitive Examinations. *J. Roy. Stat. Soc.*, 53, 460–75, 644–63.

EDWARDS, R. (1951): *Classification for Secondary Education*. Wigan: Wigan Education Committee.

EELLS, K., DAVIS, A. *et al.* (1951): *Intelligence and Cultural Differences*. Chicago, Ill.: Chicago University Press.

EMMETT, W. G. (1945): *An Enquiry into the Prediction of Grammar School Success*. London: University of London Press.

EMMETT, W. G. (1949): Evidence of a Space Factor at 11+ and Earlier. *Brit. J. Stat. Psychol.*, 2, 3–16.

EMMETT, W. G. (1954): Secondary Modern and Grammar Schools Performance Predicted by Tests given in Primary School. *Brit. J. Educ. Psychol.*, 1954, 91–8.

EMMETT, W. G. & WILMUT, F. S. (1952): The Prediction of School Certificate Performance in Specific Subjects. *Brit. J. Educ. Psychol.*, 22, 52–62.

FINLAYSON, D. S. (1951): The Reliability of Marking of Essays. *Brit. J. Educ. Psychol.*, 21, 126–34.

FLEMING, C. M. (1947–50): *Chief Examiner's Report. Kesteven and Worcestershire 1944 and 1947.* Lancashire.

FLEMING, C. M. (1952): *Research and the Basic Curriculum* (Rev. edit.). London: University of London Press.

FLEMING, C. M. (1955): *Cotswold Measurements of Ability in English and Arithmetic*, Series IX. Glasgow: Gibson.

FLOUD, J. E. (1957): Intelligence Tests, Social Class and Selection for Secondary Schools. *Brit. J. Sociol.*, 8.

FRASER, E. (1955): *Social Factors in School Progress.* Ph.D. Thesis, University of Aberdeen.

GIBSON, G. (1954): *An Enquiry into the Incidence of Coaching for the 11 Plus Examination.* M. Ed. Thesis, University of Manchester.

GLASS, D. V. (1954): *Social Mobility in Britain.* London: Routledge and Kegan Paui.

HALSEY, A. H. and GARDNER, L. (1953): Selection for Secondary Education and Achievement in Four Grammar Schools. *Brit. J. Sociol.*, 4, 60–75.

HARTOG, P. (1941): *The Marking of English Essays.* London: Macmillan.

HARTOG, P. and RHODES, E. C. (1935): *An Examination of Examinations.* London: Macmillan.

HARTOG, P., RHODES, E. C. and BURT, C. L. (1936): *The Marks of Examiners.* London: Macmillan.

HARTSHORNE, H. and MAY, M. A. (1928): *Studies in Deceit.* New York: Macmillan.

HEBB, D. O. (1949): *The Organization of Behavior.* New York: Wiley.

HEIM, A. W. (1954): *The Appraisal of Intelligence.* London: Methuen.

HEWITT, E. A. (1955): Some 11 + Rejects Who Were Subsequently Admitted to a Grammar School. *Durham. Res. Rev.*, 6, 11–17.

HIRSCH, N. D. M. (1930): Experimental Study upon Three Hundred School Children over a Six-Year Period. *Genet. Psychol. Monogr.*, 7, 487–549.

HONZIK, M. P. *et al.* (1948): The Stability of Mental Test Performances between Two and Eighteen Years. *J. Exper. Educ.*, 17, 309–24.

HUDELSON, E. (1923): English Composition: Its Aims, Methods and Measurement. *Twenty-second Yrbk. Nat. Soc. Stud. Educ.*, Pt. I.

HUSEN, T. (1950): *Testresultatens prognosvärde.* Stockholm: Gebers Vörlag.

JAMES, W. S. *et al.* (1952): *Studies in Selection Techniques for Admission to Grammar Schools.* Bristol Univ. Inst. Educ. Publ. No. 3. London: University of London Press.

KHAN, M. (1955): *A Study of the Emotional and Environmental Factors Associated with 'Backwardness' in a Seven to Eight Year Old Group of Children*. M.Sc.(Econ.) Thesis, University of London.

LAMBERT, C. M. (1949): A Survey of Ability and Interests at the Stage of Transfer. *Brit. J. Educ. Psychol.*, 19, 67–81.

LAWLEY, D. N. (1950): A Method of Standardizing Group-Tests. *Brit. J. Stat. Psychol.*, 3, 86–9.

LAWRENCE, E. M. (1931): An Investigation into the Relationship between Intelligence and Environment. *Brit. J. Psychol. Monogr. Suppl.*, No. 16.

LOVETT, T. (1956): Comprehensive Years: Progressive Differentiation. *Times Educ. Suppl.*, 27th Jan.

MCCLELLAND, W. (1942): *Selection for Secondary Education*. London: University of London Press.

MCINTOSH, D. M. (1952): Promotion of Pupils in Scotland. *Times Educ. Suppl.*, 18th July.

MCINTOSH, D. M. *et al.* (1949): *The Scaling of Teachers' Marks and Estimates*. Edinburgh: Oliver & Boyd.

MCMAHON, D. (1953): Educational Selection and Allocation. *Current Trends in British Psychology* (ed. C. A. Mace & P. E. Vernon). London: Methuen.

MILLER, W. S. (1933): Variation of I.Q.s Obtained from Group Tests. *J. Educ. Psychol.*, 24, 468–74.

MINISTRY OF EDUCATION (1954): *Report of the Central Advisory Council for Education (England): Early Leaving*. London: H.M.S.O.

MITRA, J. P. (1954): *An Analysis of Teachers' Estimates and Pupils' Performance at the Stage of Entrance to Secondary Schools*. M.A. Thesis, University of London.

MOON, A. (1955): *Educational Provision for Able Children not Selected for Grammar or Technical Schools*. M.A. Thesis, University of Birmingham.

MOORE, V. J. (1948): A Method of Allocation Used in a County Borough. *Brit. J. Educ. Psychol.*, 18, 16–20.

MORLEY, C. R. (1950): *The Problem of Age Allowances for the Selection of Children for Secondary Education at the Age of 11+*. M.A. Thesis, University of London.

MORRISON, R. L. and VERNON, P. E. (1941): A New Method of Marking English Compositions. *Brit. J. Educ. Psychol.*, 11, 109–19.

NATIONAL UNION OF TEACHERS (1949): *Transfer from Primary to Secondary Schools.* Report of Consultative Committee. London: Evans.

NEWMAN, H. H., FREEMAN, F. N. and HOLZINGER, K. J. (1937): *Twins: A Study of Heredity and Environment.* Chicago, Ill.: Chicago University Press.

NISBET, J. D. (1955): English Composition in Secondary School Selection. *Brit. J. Educ. Psychol.*, 25, 51–4.

OPPENHEIM, A. N. (1956): *A Study of the Social Attitudes of Adolescents.* Ph.D. Thesis, University of London.

PEDLEY, R. (1955): *Comprehensive Schools Today.* London: Councils and Education Press.

PEEL, E. A. (1948a): Prediction of a Complex Criterion and Battery Reliability. *Brit. J. Stat. Psychol.*, 1, 84–94.

Peel, E. A. (1948b): Assessment of Interest in Practical Topics. *Brit. J. Educ. Psychol.*, 18, 41–7.

PEEL, E. A. (1949): Evidence of a Practical Factor at the Age of Eleven. *Brit. J. Educ. Psychol.*, 19, 1–15.

PEEL, E. A. and ARMSTRONG, H. G. (1956): The Predictive Power of the English Composition in the 11 + Examination. *Brit. J. Educ. Psychol.*, 26, 163–71.

PEEL, E. A. and RUTTER, D. (1951): The Predictive Value of the Entrance Examination as Judged by the School Certificate Examination. *Brit. J. Educ. Psychol.*, 21, 30–35.

PENFOLD, A. P. (1954): *An Investigation into the Possibility of Predicting Bias towards Arts or Science in Secondary School Children.* M.A. Thesis, University of London.

PENFOLD, D. M. EDWARDS (1956): Essay Marking Experiments: Shorter and Longer Essays. *Brit. J. Educ. Psychol.*, 26, 128–36.

PIAGET, J. (1950): *The Psychology of Intelligence.* London: Routledge and Kegan Paul.

PIDGEON, D. A. and YATES, A. (1957): *Third Interim Report on the Allocation of Primary School Leavers to Courses of Secondary Education.* London: Newnes.

PILLINER, A. E. G. (1950): The Position and Size of the Borderline Group in an Examination. *Brit. J. Educ. Psychol.*, 20, 133–6.

RICHARDSON, S. C. (1956): Some Evidence Relating to the Validity of Selection for Grammar Schools. *Brit. J. Educ. Psychol.*, 26, 13–24.

RUDD, W. G. A. (1956): *The Psychological Effects of Streaming by Attainment, with Special Reference to a Group of Selected Children.* M.A. Thesis, University of London.

RUTTER, D. (1950): An Enquiry into the Predictive Value of the Grammar School Entrance Examination. *Durham Res. Rev.*, 1, 3–11.

SANDON, F. (1956): A Regression Control Chart for Use in Personnel Selection. *Appl. Stat.*, 5, 20–31.

SCHMIDT, B. G. (1946): Changes in Personal, Social and Intellectual Behaviour of Children Originally Classified as Feebleminded. *Psychol. Monogr.*, 60, No. 5.

SCOTTISH COUNCIL FOR RESEARCH IN EDUCATION (1953): *Social Implications of the 1947 Scottish Mental Survey.* London: University of London Press.

SIMON, B. (1953): *Intelligence Testing and the Comprehensive School.* London: Lawrence & Wishart.

SMITH, C. A. (1948): *Mental Testing of Hebridean Children in Gaelic and English.* London: University of London Press.

STARCH, D. (1916): *Educational Measurement.* New York: Macmillan.

STARCH, D. and ELLIOTT, E. C. (1912–13): Articles on 'The Reliability of Grading High School Work'. *School Rev.*, 20, 442–57; 21, 254–9, 676–81.

STEELE, J. H. and TALMAN, J. (1936): *The Marking of English Composition.* London: Nisbet.

SUTCLIFFE, A. and CANHAM, J. W. (1944): *Selection for Secondary Education without a Written Examination.* London: Murray.

SUTHERLAND, J. (1951): A Comparison of Pupils' Arithmetical Ability in the Secondary School with their Ability at the Time of their Transfer from Primary Schools. *Brit. J. Educ. Psychol.*, 21, 3–8.

SUTHERLAND, J. (1952): An Investigation into the Prognostic Value of Certain Arithmetic Tests at the Age of Eleven Plus. *Brit. J. Stat. Psychol.*, 5, 189–96.

TERMAN, L. M. (1916): *The Measurement of Intelligence.* London: Harrap.

TERMAN, L. M. *et al.* (1925): *Genetic Studies of Genius*, Vol. I. Stanford, Calif.: Stanford University Press.

TERMAN, L. M. *et al.* (1930): *The Promise of Youth*. Stanford, Calif.: Stanford University Press.

TERMAN, L. M. and MERRILL, M.A. (1937): *Measuring Intelligence*. London: Harrap.

TERMAN, L. M. and Oden, M. H. (1947): *The Gifted Child Grows Up*. Stanford, Calif.: Stanford University Press.

THOMSON, G. H. (1921): The Northumberland Mental Tests. *Brit. J. Psychol.*, 12, 201–22.

THOMSON, G. H. (1952): *A History of Psychology in Autobiography*, Vol. IV. Worcester, Mass.: Clark University Press.

THOMSON, G. H. and BAILES, S. M. (1926): The Reliability of Essay Marks. *Forum of Educ.*, 4, 85–91.

THORNDIKE, R. L. (1933): The Effect of the Interval between Test and Retest on the Constancy of the I.Q. *J. Educ. Psychol.*, 24, 543–9.

THORNDIKE, R. L. (1949): *Personnel Selection: Test and Measurement Techniques*. New York: Chapman & Hall.

VALENTINE, C. W. (1938): *Examinations and the Examinee*. Birmingham: Birmingham Printers.

VALENTINE, C. W. and EMMETT, W. G. (1932): *The Reliability of Examinations*. London: University of London Press.

VERNON, P. E. (1938): *The Standardization of a Graded Word Reading Test*. London: University of London Press.

VERNON, P. E. (1950): *The Structure of Human Abilities*. London: Methuen.

VERNON, P. E. (1952): *Intelligence Testing*. London: Times Publishing Co.

VERNON, P. E. (1953): *Personality Tests and Assessments*. London: Methuen.

VERNON, P. E. (1955): Letter to *Times Educ. Suppl.*, 6th May.

VERNON, P E. (1956): *The Measurement of Abilities* (Rev. edit.). London: University of London Press.

VERNON, P. E. and MILLICAN, G D. (1954): A Further Study of the Reliability of English Essays. *Brit. J. Stat. Psychol.*, 7, 65–74.

VERNON, P. E., O'GORMAN, M. and MCLELLAN, A. (1955): A Comparative Study of Educational Attainments in England and Scotland. *Brit. J. Educ. Psychol.*, 25, 195–203.

VERNON, P. E. and PARRY, J. B. (1949): *Personnel Selection in the British Forces*. London: University of London Press.

WALKER, J. (1955): Provisional Admission to Senior Secondary Courses. *Brit. J. Educ. Psychol.*, 25, 206.

WALL, W. D. (1955): *Education and Mental Health*. London: UNESCO/Harrap.

WATTS, A. F., PIDGEON, D. A. and YATES, A. (1952): *Secondary School Entrance Examinations*. London: Newnes.

WATTS, A. F. and SLATER, P. (1950): *The Allocation of Primary School Leavers to Courses of Secondary Education*. London: Newnes.

WECHSLER, D. (1949): *Intelligence Scale for Children (WISC)*. New York: Psychological Corporation.

WEST, F. (1956): The Woodlands Comprehensive School, Coventry. *Educ. Rev.*, 8, 208–17.

WISEMAN, S. (1949): The Marking of English Compositions for Grammar School Selection. *Brit. J. Educ. Psychol.*, 19, 200–9.

WISEMAN, S. (1952): *Problems Connected with the Selection of Children for Secondary Schools*. Ph.D. Thesis, University of Manchester.

WISEMAN, S. (1955): The Use of an Interest Test in 11 Plus Selection. *Brit. J. Educ. Psychol.*, 25, 92–8.

WISEMAN, S. (1956): Symposium: The Use of Essays in Selection at 11+. III. Reliability and Validity. *Brit. J. Educ. Psychol.*, 26, 172–9.

WRIGLEY, J. (1955): The Relative Efficiency of Intelligence and Attainment Tests as Predictors of Success in Grammar Schools. *Brit. J. Educ. Psychol.*, 25, 107–16.

YATES, A. (1953): Symposium on the Effects of Coaching and Practice in Intelligence Tests. I. An Analysis of Some Recent Investigations. *Brit. J. Educ. Psychol.*, 23, 147–54.

ZANGWILL, O. L. (1950): *An Introduction to Modern Psychology* London: Methuen.

Index